Table of Contents

About the Author 7

Prologue 8

Distances in kilometres/miles 9

Culmore to Coleraine (78 km) 11

Coleraine to Ballycastle (48 km) 25

Ballycastle to Larne (65 km) 42

Larne to Belfast (40 kms) 59

Belfast to Portaferry (70 kms) 69

Portaferry to Strangford (85 km) 80

Strangford to Newcastle (45 kms) 91

Newcastle to Newry (62 kms) 97

Sources 107

Acknowledgements

Several people were instrumental in both small and large ways in helping me complete my journey and write this book. My first thanks go to Mick Doherty and Declan Weafer of Motorcycle City in Dublin who have maintained and fixed my Harley-Davidson Heritage Softail motorcycle for over twelve years, and got it ready for the journey around the Causeway and Mourne Coastal Routes.

I could not have completed this task without the support and help of my family. I owe my curious mind and sense of adventure to my Dad Joe and Mum Phil who continue to inspire me to learn something new every day. To my three beautiful daughters: Claire, Kate, and Vicki – thank you for putting up with a Dad that likes big motorcycles and who spends long hours at a computer. My thanks also to Seámus Quinn, Leo Casey, David Givens, Pat Cleere, Joe O'Loughlin, Kathleen Kelleher, James Mills, and to the many friendly tour guides, publicans, restauranteurs, and museum staff who helped make my journey so enjoyable.

Finally, my greatest support and inspiration has come from my darling wife Roma. She has always stood by me and helped me to follow my dreams. Still mad about you.

Dedicated with all my love to
Roma, Claire, Kate, and Vicki.

About the Author

Dr Eugene O'Loughlin has been riding motorcycles since 1977, and has travelled widely around Ireland and Western Europe on his Harley-Davidson Heritage Softail Classic. He is a graduate of Trinity College Dublin and has worked as an educator for over 25 years. He now works as a Lecturer in Computing at the National College of Ireland where he lectures on subjects such as Business Analysis, Project Management, and Statistics. He is also a keen blogger and writes about travel, books, history, education, and technology. *Exploring Ireland's Causeway and Mourne Coastal Routes* is the second book in a trilogy of Motorcycle Odysseys following on from *Exploring Ireland's Wild Atlantic Way* published in 2014. A native of Carnew in south County Wicklow, he now lives in Dublin with his wife Roma and daughters Claire, Kate, and Vicki.

www.eugeneoloughlin.com
@eoloughlin

Prologue

In the summer of 2012 I rode my Harley-Davidson motorcycle from Kinsale in County Cork along the 2,500 kilometre Wild Atlantic Way to Muff in County Donegal. At the end of this magnificent journey I pointed the bike south to return to Dublin where I live and passed though the City of Derry when I saw signs for the Causeway Coastal Route. Despite living in Ireland for all 50 years of my life I realised that I had never been to see the Giant's Causeway or any of the other wonderful attractions on this route.

The Causeway Coastal Route, and the Mourne Coastal Route, are initiatives of the Northern Ireland Tourist Board to attract visitors to the wonderful 500 kilometre coastline that runs around the counties of Derry, Antrim, and Down. It includes the famous World Heritage Site at the Giant's Causeway, curiosities like the Carrick-a-Rede Rope Bridge, cosmopolitan cities like Derry and Belfast, historic links to the past with St Patrick, the Titanic, and World War II, plus the splendour of the Mountains of Mourne. There is much to see and do in Northern Ireland where tourism has undergone a massive boost in the last twenty years.

The road that runs from Derry to Newry right around the Northern Ireland coast is the A2, which I would get to know very well over the next few days. In many places the road is carved out of the cliff edges to give a unique experience of long stretches of riding right along the shore line. A motorcycle is an ideal way to tour these two coastal routes, but they are also popular with cyclists and people who drive in cages (cars).

So, with no set plan to achieve a certain distance each day, or any destination in mind, I set out from Dublin to Muff in County Donegal to start a new motorcycle odyssey where the Wild Atlantic Way ends, and the Causeway Coastal Route begins.

Distances in kilometres/miles

Distances are measured in kilometres throughout this book. The tables below show the distances for each section of the Causeway and Mourne Coastal Routes in both kilometres and miles.

Causeway Coastal Route

	Kilometres	Miles
Culmore to Coleraine	78	49
Coleraine to Ballycastle	48	30
Ballycastle to Larne	65	40
Larne to Belfast	40	25

Mourne Coastal Route

	Kilometres	Miles
Belfast to Portaferry	70	43
Portaferry to Strangford	85	53
Strangford to Newcastle	45	28
Newcastle to Newry	62	39

Culmore to Coleraine (78 km)

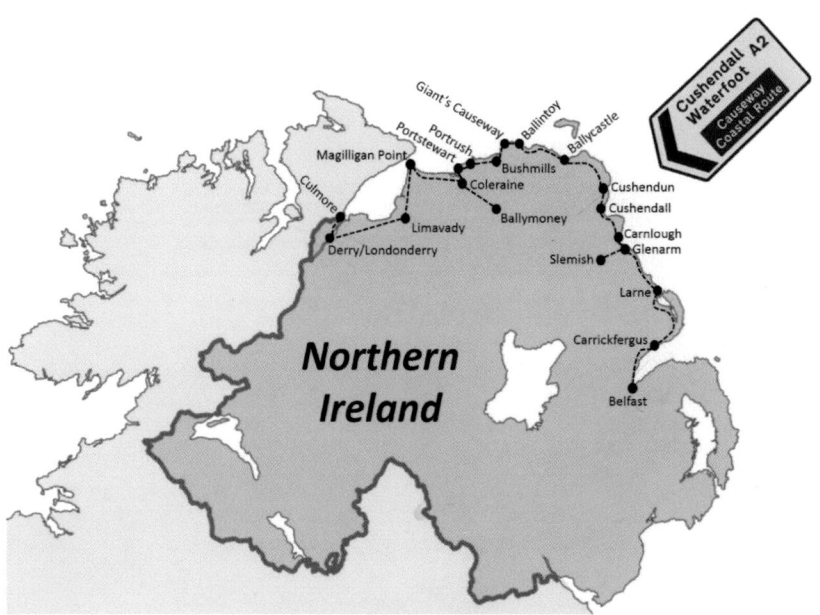

The Causeway Coastal Route.

The starting point for my journey around the Northern Ireland Coastline was at the Donegal/Derry border which marks the beginning of the 230km Causeway Coastal Route. Ahead of me and my bike lay historic cities, towns, and villages along one of the best motorcycle riding routes in Europe. The first part of the journey is the short road from the border to Derry city, but on the way I took a detour down to Culmore Point on Lough Foyle. Here there is a tower castle, now used by the Lough Foyle Yacht Club, which has an interesting background. The tower is all that is left of a larger castle which was fortified by Sir Henry Docwra in the year 1600. Sir Henry is also known as 'the founder of Derry', and he was sent to Ireland to subdue this part of the island during the rebellion by the Irish against the English known as the Nine Years War (1594-1603).

The castle was later seized by Sir Cahir O'Doherty in another rebellion in 1608 who then went on to sack and burn Derry city. Despite its violent past, the tower is situated in a peaceful place with only the occasional family of swans and ships passing up and down Lough Foyle to disturb this pleasant setting. Culmore is also the location where on 20 May 1932 the famous aviator Emelia Earhart landed after the first solo transatlantic flight by a woman. She had left Newfoundland in Canada flying a Lockheed Vega 5B intending to land in Paris, but after almost 15 hours of flying bad weather forced her to land in Culmore. The Amelia Earhart Centre in nearby Ballygarnett Country Park is a small museum that tells the story of her unexpected landing in Culmore.

O'Doherty's Castle, Culmore Point

Leaving Culmore it is a short ride to Derry city where I head straight for the tourist office on Foyle Street near the walled city centre. Here I collect many leaflets and lots of information about touring Northern Ireland. The extremely helpful and knowledgeable staff

Culmore to Coleraine

recommended that I try out a walking tour of the nearby city walls. I had never been to this historic city before so I set out with lots of other tourists to walk the walls.

A swan family at Lough Foyle

Our tour guide first explained how the city and county were named. The official name of the city today is Londonderry. The ancient name was Derry Calgach, meaning oak wood of Calgach. St Columkille, who was from nearby Donegal, built a monastery in Derry in the year 546, and in the tenth century this area was known as Derry Columkille. This continued to the time of King James I who granted a charter in 1604 and the name changed to Londonderry in honour of the London business people who helped finance the development of the city. The use of either Londonderry or Derry as the name of the city and county still causes debate, and some confusion, to this day. Many efforts are made to avoid using either name, for example the local parliamentary constituency name is 'Foyle'.

A walk around the walls of Derry is a must for anyone visiting this city which was named the first ever UK City of Culture in 2013. The walls make up the only complete walled city on the island of Ireland and is one of the few examples of its type in Europe. Many historians trace the founding of Derry back to the year 1600 when Sir Henry Docwra landed at Culmore and made his way to what we now know as Derry. He fortified battlements and built streets and by 1603 Derry was granted city status.

The walls were built during the period 1613-1618 as a protection for new settlers from England and Scotland. As our tour party walked along the top of the 1.5 kilometre long walls, our guide gave us fascinating accounts of the 105 day siege of Derry in 1688 when the armies of King James II failed to capture the city which was defended resolutely with shouts of 'No Surrender'. Many of the cannons used to defend the city are placed along the walls.

Cannon on the Walls of Derry.

You get an intense sense of history when you stand beside these huge machines of destruction and wonder what it must have been like to be up on the walls firing down at King James' soldiers, or to be outside the city facing cannon fire from the walls. We stood for a long time at the western section of the walls which overlooks the area known as the Bogside. Our guide told us about The Troubles, but that Derry is a much different city now since the violence ended. Later I would go down to the streets of the Bogside to see them for myself, but for now I try to imagine what stories these walls could tell since they were built 400 years ago.

Our tour ends at The Diamond in the centre of the walled city. This is now a busy shopping area bustling with locals and tourists. At the centre of The Diamond is a magnificent war memorial built in 1927 to commemorate the citizens of Derry who lost their lives in the two World Wars. At the top of the cenotaph shaped monument is a winged victory statue, and at the foot are two statues representing the army and the navy. This was to be the first of many war memorials I would see in the towns of Northern Ireland during my journey around its coastline. World war memorials such as these are rare in the Republic of Ireland, but I think it is important to remember tragic events like war that might be difficult to speak about but which are impossible to be silent on.

Overlooking the Bogside.

Back on the bike I rode the short distance around to what is known as Free Derry Corner on Rossville Street in the Bogside. This place is steeped in tragedy and hope at the same time. The first thing you will notice is the iconic gable wall bearing the slogan 'You Are Now Entering Free Derry'. This was reputedly first painted on this wall by a man called

John 'Caker' Casey in 1969, though there is some dispute about who actually created the slogan. A small plaque at the side of the wall commemorates Casey, who died in the year 2000, as the man who painted the slogan. Nowadays the wall is regularly repainted and is often used to support causes such as Sarcoma Awareness.

Free Derry Corner at Rossville Street.

All along Rossville Street is a series of twelve murals painted by the Bogside Artists group. These murals bear witness to the troubled times past in Derry, and this series of wall paintings are one of the top tourist attractions in Derry. They commemorate episodes from The Troubles such as the Hunger Strikes, Bloody Sunday, and the Civil Rights campaign. They also pay tribute to the well-known Derry politicians John Hume and Bernadette Devlin McAliskey. But for me the most iconic and moving murals were those showing a 'Petrol Bomber' and 'Death of Innocence'. The petrol bomber mural depicts a scene from the 'Battle of the Bogside' in 1969. The death of innocence mural shows a painting of 14-year old Annette McGavigan who was shot dead in 1971 when she went with friends to collect rubber bullets that littered the

Culmore to Coleraine

ground after a riot - she was the 100th civilian to be killed in The Troubles and was also the first child to die. This evocative mural of a school girl will stay in the mind of any visitor to Derry for a long time.

The 'Petrol Bomber' mural.

It was time to leave Derry and set out for the rest of the Causeway Coastal Route. On my way I stop at the Peace Bridge that joins the two sides of Derry - the Cityside on the west of the Foyle River and Waterside on the east. This snaking bridge is 235 metres long and is designed for pedestrians and cyclists only. Further south is Derry's oldest bridge which is known as the Craigavon Bridge. It was completed in 1933 and replaced the older Carlisle Bridge which was built in 1862 after the previous wooden bridge was destroyed by an iceberg. Craigavon Bridge, named in honour of Lord Craigavon who was the first Prime Minister of Northern Ireland, is one of the few double-decker road bridges in Europe. I take the A2 road out of Derry, much of this road will be my companion for the next few days. With fond memories of my short visit to Derry city I ride north towards Magilligan Point.

Exploring Northern Ireland's Causeway and Mourne Coastal Routes

The Causeway Coastal Route does not directly pass through the town of Limavady as a bypass will steer you away from the town centre. However, do remember as you pass by that one of the most famous tunes ever was written here in 1851 - the 'Londonderry Air'. Limavady native, Jane Ross, reputedly wrote down the notes of the air which she heard being played by a blind fiddler opposite her house on market day. In 1913 English lyricist Fred Weatherly added words to the tune and the world famous song 'Danny Boy' was born. The seacoast road from Limavady to Magilligan runs along by the River Roe through a mostly flat landscape. This is a very easy ride and the views from the road are made easier to see by the well-trimmed hedges that line the road.

Binevenagh Mountain.

Soon after leaving Limavady, Binevenagh Mountain starts to dominate the views and surrounding landscape. This mountain has a basalt cliff-like face looking west and has been designated as both an Area of Special Scientific Interest and an Area of Outstanding Natural Beauty by the Northern Ireland Environment Agency because of its geological and geomorphological features. It marks the end of the

Culmore to Coleraine

Antrim Plateau which is made up of basalt that forms after volcanic lava cools.

I made my way towards Magilligan Point where there is a small harbour that provides a ferry service to Greencastle in County Donegal from April to October. The crossing only takes about 10 minutes, but will save tourists a 1.5 hour drive around Lough Foyle through Derry to get to the Inishowen Peninsula on the other side of the lough. An interesting feature here is the Martello Tower that overlooks Lough Foyle. It is one of the best preserved of the 40 surviving such towers on the Irish coast. It was built in 1812 to control the narrow mouth of Lough Foyle at this point against the threat from Napoleon. Martello Towers are named after a fort at Mortella Point in Corsica which successfully withstood bombardment by the British Navy in 1794. During the World War II the tower had a pillbox fitted on top, though no shots were ever fired in anger from this position.

Martello Tower, Magilligan Point.

Another major landmark near here is the more modern, and rather bleak looking Magilligan Prison. It is due to close in 2018 and is classified as a medium security prison. With all the high fences and barbed wire I felt it was definitely better to be on the outside looking in.

The area around the prison is a nature reserve and a firing range for the British Army. The many 'Military Firing Range - Keep Out' signs along the road make sure that curious bikers and other tourists do not stray onto this dangerous location.

Leaving the Magilligan I head directly eastwards across the coast of County Derry. The Seacoast Road ends at the tiny village of Downhill situated at the end Benone Beach which stretches for just over 11 kilometres westwards back to Magilligan Point, one of the longest beaches in Ireland. From some distance away as you approach Downhill you can see a tower perched on the edge of a cliff. Among the remarkable features of the Causeway Coastal Route are the castles that crown its cliffs. The first of these that I came across is the Mussenden Temple, which is part of the Downhill Demesne that is now a park run by the National Trust. I entered the park through the Lion's Gate and parked the bike as all the paths here are pedestrian only. I walked first up to the fantastic ruin of Downhill House. I'm sure that like everyone else who comes here for the first time, I wondered at what the house must have been like in its prime.

Ruins of Downhill House.

Culmore to Coleraine

Downhill House was built in the early 1770s by the Earl of Bristol, Frederick Hervey, who had become Bishop of Derry in 1768. Quite why he chose this location so close to the sea is both bewildering and inspired. One early visitor said of the house that he had 'never seen so bad a house occupy as much ground', while another called it 'a sad monument of human folly'. However, today it makes for a spectacular location to visit. Sadly, the house was destroyed by fire in 1851 during which several pieces of art collected by Hervey were lost. It was rebuilt in 1874 by the Bruce family who lived in the house until the 1920s. It was taken over by the Royal Air Force during the Second World War after which the roof was removed and the house dismantled leaving only the bare walls that stand today. You can walk through all the rooms, which are labelled by the National Trust, to get an idea of what it must have been like to live in.

On the northern side of the house there is a path leading straight to the cliffs where the beautiful Mussenden Temple draws you towards the sea. Situated 36.5 metres above the shore and sitting directly on top of a railway line, the temple remains one of Northern Ireland's most iconic attractions. It was built in 1785 as a summer library and it's modelled on the Temple of Vesta in Rome. It was intended as a refuge for Frederick Hervey's married cousin Frideswide Mussenden, with whom it was said he was infatuated with. However, she died shortly after it was completed and it then became a memorial to her. Around the top of the temple is an inscription in Latin that translates as:

> *Tis pleasant, safely to behold from shore*
> *The rolling ship, and hear the tempest roar*

Leaving the Downhill and Mussenden Demesne I stopped briefly at the nearby Hezlett House which is located at the corner of the junction leading to the seaside village of Castlerock. It is one of the oldest thatched dwellings in Ireland dating from 1690, though it was not until 1766 that the Hezlett family made it their home. In its tiny rooms you can learn about the reality of life in the late seventeenth century, the cottage is also home to the Downhill Marbles collection. In 1976 the cottage was sold by the Hezletts to the National Trust who now maintain it as a museum.

Exploring Northern Ireland's Causeway and Mourne Coastal Routes

Mussenden Temple.

The village of Castlerock is a popular seaside holiday destination. It was here that the writer C.S. Lewis came on holiday when he was young and it is thought that he found inspiration for some of his books here, including the first novel of his Chronicles of Narnia series, 'The Lion, the Witch and the Wardrobe' published in 1950. Castlerock is where Northern Ireland's longest river, the Bann, meets the sea. It rises 159 kilometres away in the Mourne Mountains and flows through Lough Neagh, the largest lake in Ireland. The Bann estuary, known as Barmouth, is a Special Site of Scientific Interest and a National Trust Nature Reserve where wild fowl and wading birds share this area with some of the rarest coastal plants and flowers on the island of Ireland.

Dunlop Memorial Garden, Ballymoney.

By now it was early evening and time to finish touring for the day, so I headed towards Coleraine to stay the night. As there is no bridge over the river Bann estuary, I rode inland through the village of Articlave and the surrounding green fields, to cross the Bann in Coleraine. Before settling for the evening there was one more trip to make. Ballymoney, just 12 kilometres from Coleraine, was the home of motorcycle racing legends, Joey and Robert Dunlop. So I paid a visit to the Memorial Garden on Castle Street named after two of Northern Ireland's most famous sons. This is a must stop location for any motorcyclist and the fine memorial features statues of the two brothers and a list of all their race wins. Both died tragically while riding their bikes. Joey died during a

125cc race in Estonia in 2000 after crashing into a tree. Eight years later in 2008 Robert died during practice for the North West 200, a race he had won a record 15 times. Despite this tragedy, his son Michael took part in the race and won, dedicating his victory to his Dad. Today the peaceful garden is regularly disturbed by the noise of motorcycle engines from fans who want to visit the garden and pay their respects to the Dunlop brothers.

Coleraine to Ballycastle (48 km)

The town of Coleraine was my starting point for day two of my journey around the Causeway Coastal Route. I took a walk around the town centre before the shops opened and almost had the quiet streets to myself. The pedestrianized centre of the town is called 'The Diamond' and has the Town Hall as a centrepiece. This hall was first built in 1743, re-built in 1859, and was restored to its current glory in 1995 following a bomb attack.

Coleraine Town Hall

At the front of the hall is a war memorial to local men who gave their lives during both world wars. Lots of flowers decorate the memorial and once again I am impressed by the dedication of local people in Northern Ireland to commemorate their war dead. I feel certain that if I was a young man in 1914 that I too would have 'joined up' and might have ended up named on a memorial somewhere.

Bertie Peacock, Coleraine.

Coleraine to Ballycastle

Close by the Town Hall is a fine statue to one of Northern Ireland's football heroes - Bertie Peacock. He played for both Coleraine in the Irish League and Glasgow Celtic in the Scottish League. His most famous achievements were that he was part of the Northern Ireland team that reached the quarter finals of the World Cup in 1958, and that as manager of the national team picked the legendary George Best for his first international appearance. He was also assistant manager to Billy Bingham during Northern Ireland's famous 1982 World Cup campaign in Spain.

Portstewart Strand.

It was still a cool early morning when I left Coleraine in the direction of Portstewart, one of Northern Ireland's most popular holiday resorts. With a beautiful 3 kilometre long strand it is easy to see why people flock to this seaside town. Even though it was still quite early there were already many cars parked on the sand and people walking the strand. I dared not try my bike on the strand and parked at the end of the road. From the strand you can see as far as the Inishowen peninsula in Donegal and if you walk westwards you will eventually reach the Bann

Estuary. The Mussenden Temple can still be seen dominating the cliff edge over-looking the early morning walkers. This strand has been recognised in 2014 as one of the twelve best beaches in the United Kingdom by the Rough Guides website, and it is easy to see why. It is a perfect place to spend a day at the beach taking long walks and exploring the dunes that separate the strand from Portstewart Golf Club.

There have been many ship wrecks off the coast of Northern Ireland. Perhaps the most famous near Portstewart was the 549 ton American square rigger, called the *George A. Hopley*, which was driven onto the Portstewart Strand in July 1856. It carried a cargo of rum and cloth worth £66,000, a huge sum at the time. Some of this cargo is reputed to be buried in the nearby dunes for safe-keeping. Also just 11 kilometres north of Portstewart is the wreck of a German U-boat which was scuttled following a collision with the Canadian warship the *New Glasgow*.

Antrim Gardens, Portrush.

Portrush is located on Ramore Head which juts out to the sea. I stopped at the small Antrim Gardens overlooking a string of seventeen small rocky islands called the Skerries, which are the remains of volcanic activities from long ago. Before the harbour was built in Portrush, these islands offered some shelter for shipping. The Skerries is a designated Area of Special Scientific Interest, and a National Nature Reserve. At the centre of the Antrim Gardens is an interesting red brick sculpture modelled in a lighthouse. It depicts the history of Portrush and shows images of Vikings, the Spanish Armada, and traders in Clipper Ships.

The short 6 kilometre road from Portstewart to Portrush is a pleasant ride that runs along the coastline past many holiday homes and caravan parks. This road also marks the end my journey around County Derry as I cross into County Antrim. The old Gaelic name for this region was *Aentruibh*, which probably means either 'one tribe' or 'one habitation', but it is not certain if this is the origin of the name.

Welcome to Portrush.

I stopped at the hill overlooking Portrush Harbour where there is a sign welcoming visitors to the 'Major Golf Capital of the World'. They are very proud here that from such a small town hailed winners of the 1947 British Open (Fred Daly), the 2010 US Open (Graeme McDowell), and the 2011 British Open (Darren Clarke). The Royal Portrush Golf Club boasts two championship courses: the Dunluce Links, and the

Exploring Northern Ireland's Causeway and Mourne Coastal Routes

Valley Links. The British Open was held in Royal Portrush in 1951, the only time it has been held outside England or Scotland since the Open began in 1860. In 2014 it was announced that the Open is soon to return to Royal Portrush, possibly in 2019.

There's more to Portrush than golf, and I parked the bike beside the harbour to take a look around. It is thought that there has been some kind of settlement in this area since the twelfth century, but it was not until the mid-seventeenth century that a fishing village was established. It only became a popular holiday resort after the arrival of the railway in 1855. With the nearby Giant's Causeway as a major local attraction, Portrush grew to become one of the major holiday resort towns in Ireland.

Dunluce Castle.

A short ride of 5 kilometres along the A2 after Portrush are probably the most picturesque ruins in Ireland at Dunluce Castle. As with the Mussenden Temple, it is elegantly perched on top of a cliff overlooking the sea. It is just a short walk from the road and even though it was just mid-morning already there were many tourists wandering around this unusual attraction. The castle was originally built by Richard de Burgh, the 2nd Earl of Ulster, in the thirteenth century. He was also known as the Red Earl of Ulster and another interesting fact about him is that his daughter became the second wife of Robert the Bruce who became King of Scotland in 1306. The castle subsequently belonged to the McQuillan clan who lost the castle to the wonderfully named Sorley Boy McDonnell in 1583. Sorley Boy was born in 1505 in Scotland, and lived to the remarkable old age for the time of 85 years. One of the most tragic events following the disaster of the Spanish Armada occurred here when the galleon 'La Girona' with 1,300 men on board was wrecked against the rocks here. Only nine survived and were sent to Scotland by Sorley Boy for safety. He also helped himself to four cannons, which he mounted on the castle walls, and two chests of treasure from the wreck. After the mid-1700s the castle fell into ruins.

The Bushmills Distillery.

Lying in the fields outside Dunluce castle gates are the buried remains of the lost village of Dunluce which was thought to have been founded in 1608 by Randall McDonnell, who went on to become the first Earl of Antrim in 1620. The village was destroyed by fire in 1642 and gradually faded out of existence as a village by the 1680s. Since then the village's buildings decayed and collapsed until they became lost beneath the green fields we see today, Dunluce is sometimes called 'Little Pompeii' as a result. Archaeologists have recently discovered that this 'village' is older than was originally thought. Excavations by the Northern Ireland Environment Agency have revealed that Dunluce village existed in the late 1400s and even had cobbled streets. Archaeological work is continuing to establish the extent of the village.

Leaving Dunluce Castle I made my way through the green fields of Ulster towards the town of Bushmills. The town gets its name from the River Bush and a large watermill that was once located here. The town centre features a war memorial with a lone statue of a rifleman with fixed bayonet at the ready. The memorial has 87 names of men, mostly from Royal Irish Rifles regiments. Bushmills is of course world famous for the Irish Whiskey of the same name that is distilled here, and I made my way to the distillery which is also a visitor attraction. Whiskey has been distilled here since 1608 when King James I granted Sir Thomas Phillips a license to distil - making it the oldest licensed distillery in the world. Tours are available and you can see each room where whiskey is mixed, fermented, distilled, stored in casks, and finally bottled. Finally a tasting room will make you leave with a smile!

At the Giant's Causeway.

Arguably the greatest feature on the coast of Northern Ireland is the Giant's Causeway which is just 4 kilometres away from Bushmills. By now there was a lot of traffic on the road with hundreds of people looking to see what is sometimes called the Eighth Wonder of the World. Tourists have marvelled at the mystery and magic of the Giant's Causeway for centuries and it is recognised as a World Heritage Site by UNESCO. The Causeway is just a three hour bike ride from my home in Dublin, but I had never been here before. There is a great new Centre with a large car park where the attendants offered to mind my bike and gear. As it is a bit of a hike from the Centre down to the Causeway I was glad to be able to leave my leather jacket and helmet on the bike in safe hands. Nothing prepares you for the natural wonder that awaits at the sea shore where over 40,000 black basalt columns stick out of the sea. With formations that have names like 'Camel's Hump', the 'Chimney Stacks', the 'Harp', and the 'Organ', there are wonders at every turn.

Columns of basalt known as 'Chimney Stacks'.

Sixty million years ago this part of County Antrim was subject to intense volcanic activity. Highly fluid molten lava was forced up through cracks in the chalk bed to form the extensive Antrim Plateau. As the lava cooled, columns of mostly six-sided rocks were formed. Of course legend has it that the causeway was created in a much more dramatic way. The Irish giant Finn McCool, reputedly 16 metres tall, built the

Causeway from Antrim to Scotland as stepping stones to fight the Scottish giant Benandonner. After Finn built the Causeway he was tired and went to sleep. Benandonner arrived from Scotland for the fight, but when Finn's wife Oonagh saw how big the Scottish giant was she covered Finn with a blanket. Benandonner roared 'where's Finn?' and looked at the sleeping Finn. Oonagh told him to 'be quiet, or you'll wake the bairn'. With this, Benandonner panicked - if the child (bairn) was this big, how much bigger must the father be? He hastily retreated across the stepping stones back home to Scotland, destroying the Causeway on the way. I prefer this story to imagining what molten lava cooling looked like!

A view of the Giant's Causeway.

Hundreds of people were climbing all over the rocks and looking in awe at the formations. Cameras were clicking and beeping everywhere and no doubt there are thousands of 'selfies' and photos for everyone to treasure a memorable visit to the Giant's Causeway. Before leaving I shopped in the Visitor Centre for a few souvenirs. Much educational information about the Causeway is also provided here in audio-visual displays. About half a million tourists visit here every year and everything is extremely well organised and managed for the visitor. It was with a reluctant heart that I left what for me is the most wonderful site on the island of Ireland. Once you visit the Giant's Causeway you will never ever forget it!

Riding eastwards I came across the ruins of Dunseverick Castle beside a small natural harbour. This site is easy to reach as it is well signposted and is beside the A2 road. All that remains today are the ruins of the castle's gate lodge to the left of the little inlet. The castle is located at the end of one of the ancient royal roads from the seat of the Irish High Kings in Tara. St Patrick is also reputed to have carried out baptisms here - I imagine walking in the footsteps of our patron saint who visited this location on several occasions. The castle was destroyed by the Scottish General Robert Munro in 1642 following the Irish Rebellion in 1641. For good measure it was finished off in 1652 by Cromwellian troops. Just 1 kilometre further along the road is the tiny Dunseverick Harbour which is at the end of a short twisty road. The harbour is still in use by local fishermen, and this is also a good location for tourists to know about as in addition to some lovely views and walks, there are toilet facilities here too.

Ruins of Dunseverick Castle.

Exploring Northern Ireland's Causeway and Mourne Coastal Routes

Leaving Dunseverick I stopped at the nearby White Bay Viewpoint which overlooks a fine beach and the tiny village of Portbraddan. It is here where you will see St Gobban's church, reputedly at about 2.5 metres by 1 metre in size, the smallest church in Ireland. The village was once known as a salmon station - indeed the name of the village is taken from the Irish for 'Port of Salmon', and the views around here are very picturesque. The cliff-like Bengore Head juts out in to the sea towards the west, while you can clearly see the Isle of Islay in Scotland to the north. Towards the east I caught my first glimpse of Rathlin Island.

White Bay overlooking Portbraddan.

Earlier on my trip when I was getting petrol in Derry, I got chatting with a man who was admiring my Harley-Davidson. I told him about my upcoming trip around Northern Ireland's coast and he urged me not to miss the 'crackin' little harbour at Ballintoy. Despite the world renowned sites along this coastline I decided to take a brief stop at this harbour and I was not disappointed! The harbour is at the end of a twisty section of narrow road and despite a huge amount of traffic, it is worth the effort to go and see. This harbour once did a thriving trade with Scotland, which is only 40 kilometres away across the sea. Two industries were based here. The first was the production of sett (paving) stones which were used to pave streets in Dublin, Cork, Wexford, Limerick, and Glasgow. The second industry was the burning of lime in a huge lime kiln which still exists. The lime was used to neutralize the acid soil on inland farms. Also of interest here is a large cave at the end of the car park which in the past was used to repair boats.

Ballintoy Harbour.

Ballintoy Harbour was also used in the TV series 'Game of Thrones', based on the 'Song of Ice and Fire' books by George R.R. Martin. The harbour was refitted to look like the Iron Island from the book, and is just one of many locations in Northern Ireland used in the TV series. One of the most iconic locations, the Dark Hedges, is located just 14 kilometres inland from Ballintoy at Gracehill House near the village of Armoy, so I took a quick detour from the Causeway Coastal Route to check it out. The Dark Hedges is actually a road lined with beech trees leading up to Gracehill House, and was created in the eighteenth century as an impressive entrance by the Stuart family who lived in Gracehill. Beech trees reach maturity after about 150 to 200 years, and many are already older than this. Several old and diseased trees have recently been felled or trimmed for safety reasons. Even before the Game of Thrones TV series, the Dark Hedges were well known, but today is even more popular with visitors. It is no wonder that this mystical location has been included as one of the 12 best road trips in Ireland and the UK by the Continental Road Trip website.

The Dark Hedges.

Yet another famous tourist attraction along the Causeway Coastal Route is the Carrick-a-Rede rope bridge which is just 2.5 kilometres from Ballintoy Harbour. The rope bridge is 20 metres long and is 30 metres above the rocks below. The current bridge was put in place in 2008 by the National Trust, replacing an older less safe version. It connects the mainland to the small Carrickarede Island created 60 million years ago by volcanic eruptions. As it was early afternoon when I arrived the place was very crowded with tourists. There is quite a bit of a walk from the ticket office to the bridge, and with no security at the bike park I had no choice but to carry my leather jacket with me. Be warned - at busy times like this there are long queues to cross the bridge. Crossing is done in groups in one direction at a time. The National Trust stewards keep everybody moving and soon I was on the small island of Carrickarede.

Coleraine to Ballycastle

While many tourists who crossed the bridge immediately joined the queue to get back across, I and many others sampled to great views from the island. To the west were the distinctive Ulster chalk cliffs, while to the north were views of Rathlin Island and the Mull of Kintyre in Scotland beyond. To the east I could see Fair Head in the distance. On a beautiful sunny day like this it is the best way to enjoy the Causeway Coastal Route.

Carrick-a-Rede Rope Bridge.

One of the largest towns on the North Antrim coast is Ballycastle where I stop for a late lunch at The Marconi Bar overlooking the harbour. Here I had just about the best seafood chowder I have ever had, and great hospitality too. Ballycastle Harbour is also the location of the ferry to Rathlin Island which is just 10 kilometres away. A plaque overlooking the harbour commemorates the 'world's first commercial radio signal' between Marconi stations on Rathlin Island and in Ballycastle on 6 July 1898. This world 'first' is disputed as there were similar signals recorded in 1897 in Bristol in England.

Ballycastle lies in a beautiful setting when on a clear day you can see the Mull of Kintyre in Scotland out to sea. Overlooking the town is the 517 metre Knocklayde Mountain, and you can just about make out the small mound on the top known as the 'Cairn of Sorrow'. Ballycastle is the location for the ferry to and from Rathlin Island. The island is home to about 125 people and has an unusual L-shape. It is almost 10 kilometres long and 1.5 kilometres wide, and is the most northerly point in Northern Ireland. Legend has it that it is supposed to owe its existence to the mother of the giant Finn McCool. Once when Finn drank all the whiskey in Ireland, his mother travelled to Scotland to get some more and brought a mountain with her to use as a stepping stone. However, she tripped and dropped the mountain into the sea, and so it became Rathlin Island.

Children of Lir sculpture over Fair Head at Ballycastle sea front, with Mull of Kintyre in the background.

On the sea front promenade looking out towards Fair Head there is a beautiful sculpture of four flying swans depicting The Children of Lir who, according to Irish legend, were transformed into birds by a jealous stepmother. The legend tells us that the swans spent a winter at the mouth of the nearby River Margy. At the other side of the harbour is a similar sculpture depicting the various types of local fish called 'Leap of Faith' - both sculptures were created by Malcolm Robertson from

Coleraine to Ballycastle

Scotland. The promenade and harbour are well worth stopping at for a walk and I certainly enjoyed my visit to Ballycastle.

Motorcycles at Carrick-a-Rede.

Ballycastle to Larne (65 km)

When the Giro d'Italia bicycle road race came to Northern Ireland in 2014, it also became a tour within a tour by circling around the county of Antrim. From Ballycastle to Larne, most of the Giro route ran along the Antrim coast and I set out to follow the tire tracks of my motorcycle's two-wheeled cousins. It was not by accident that this route was chosen as it show-cased some of Northern Ireland's most beautiful scenery. There are many reminders that the Giro passed through County Antrim with pink decorations all along the route. Flower pots, old bicycles, and gates were all painted pink in honour of the 'Maglia Rosa' (Pink Jersey), worn by the race leader of the Giro.

Lough na Cranagh at Fair Head.

Leaving Ballycastle riding across North Antrim the Giro cyclists will have had wonderful views towards Fair Head. This cliff-like headland rises 196m above the sea, which makes it very popular with climbers, it is believed to be the largest expanse of vertical climbable rock in either Britain or Ireland. Unfortunately you can't ride up to the top, but you can get close by road. The effort to walk to the top of the Head is definitely worth it as there is a small lake, called Lough na Cranagh, with an island in the middle surrounded by a low wall. This is a 'crannóg', or an artificial island refuge, of which there are an estimated 1,200 on the island of Ireland built since about 600 AD. I continued to the top of Fair Head where there are specular views of the North Antrim coast, with brilliant views towards Rathlin Island and Knocklayde Mountain, and on a clear day to many parts of Scotland.

The cliff face at Fair Head.

Fair Head, and the nearby Murlough Bay, is a very popular walk for hikers. The story of how Fair Head was named was given to me by one hiker. Legend has it that the King of Rathlin Island arranged for his beautiful fair-haired daughter to marry a Viking Chief as a peace settlement. However, she was already in love with another, which not surprisingly angered the Viking who was struck by her beauty. A great feast was organised on top of the head and the jealous Viking bribed a servant to push her over the edge while dancing. When her devastated father found her body at the foot of the cliff the next day he decreed that the location be known from that time forward as Fair Head in honour of his daughter.

The Vanishing Lake at Loughareema.

Probably the most unusual sight that any of the Giro d'Italia cyclists from all over the world will ever see from their bikes is the Vanishing Lake at Loughareema, which is just 10 kilometres from Ballycastle. The lake is beside the road and is known to empty and fill rapidly - geologists are not certain why this is the case. The lake had vanished when I arrived at this location. Generally it is thought that because Loughareema sits on a bed of Ulster chalk there is a 'plug hole' that gets blocked with peat, when this happens the lake fills up. When the plug is cleared, all the water in the lake drains underground, reportedly at a rapid rate. Another curiosity about this lake is that it is supposed to be haunted! In 1898 a local man named Colonel John Magee McNeille misjudged the depth of the lake's waters when the road was flooded while rushing for a train in Ballycastle in his horse-drawn wagon. He persuaded his coach driver to drive the wagon through the water, but when they reached the middle, the cold water reached the horses' bellies and made them nervous. The coach driver used his whip, which caused the horses to rear up. As a consequence all fell into the water and the colonel, his coach driver, and the two horses were drowned. Visitors are warned that on nights when the lake is full, a ghostly coach and passengers haunt the lake shores.

The A2 in North Antrim.

From Loughareema back to the coast of East Antrim, the Causeway Coastal Route runs through the bleak but picturesque landscape on the road to Cushendun. There were lots of green fields, forests, and heather covered hills either side of the narrow but straight A2 road. This is all part of the Antrim Coast and Glens Area of Outstanding Natural Beauty. This area encompasses the coastline from Ballycastle to Larne in the south of the county. It also includes Rathlin Island and continues inland to the Glens of Antrim and the Antrim Plateau.

Arriving in Cushendun I was immediately struck by the black and white themed cottages that make up a lot of this picturesque National Trust Preserved village. These were built in the style of similar Cornish villages designed by architect Clough Williams-Ellis, who designed similar villages in Stowe and Tattenhall in England, and Portmeirion in

Wales. A brick-walled bridge over the Glendun River connects the two sides of the village, the bridge looks quite new as it was repaired in 2010 at great inconvenience to transport and the locals.

Johann the Goat at the mouth of the Glendun River, Cushendun.

At the end of the bridge is an interesting sculpture of a goat by Northern Irish sculptor Deborah Brown. As the sign on the sculpture tells us it was erected in 2002 in honour of Johann the goat who was the unfortunate last animal to be culled during a Foot and Mouth Disease outbreak in Ireland during 2001. Overall, nearly 51,000 animals in Northern Ireland were culled during this outbreak. Added to the 53,000 culled in the south of Ireland, this was a terrible disaster to hit agriculture on this island. The tiny harbour here was also the location of a regular ferry service between Cushendun and the Mull of Kintyre in Scotland from the mid-1600s until it ceased during the Great Famine in the 1840s.

Cushendun also marks the end of one of the famous Nine Glens of Antrim - Glendun. The others are: Glenarm, Glencloy, Glenariff, Glenballyeamon, Glenaan, Glencorp, Glenshesk, and Glentaisie. These glens were carved by retreating glaciers during the Ice Age thousands of years ago. Today they are a major tourist attraction with each glen having its own unique character. The northern most glen of Glendun is also known for a viaduct further inland from the coast. Built in 1839 as part of what was called William Bald's Antrim Coast Road, it is not that easy to see from the road. It is considered a classic amongst viaducts and was designed by the English architect Charles Lanyon, who was also responsible for the designs of some of the buildings in Queen's University as well as Crumlin Road Gaol and Courthouse in Belfast. Later on this trip in Belfast I would visit the Lanyon designed Victorian gaol, and also see a castle designed by him in Killyleagh.

Leaving Cushendun I travelled along the 8 kilometre road to the Capital of the Glens of Antrim at Cushendall. On entering the village I stopped at a fine mural which depicts three of what Cushendall is most proud of: the local Ruairí Óg GAA club, the Curfew Tower, and Lurigethan Mountain. Gaelic games have always been played in many parts of County Antrim. The Ruairí Óg club was founded in 1906 and is one of the county's most successful GAA clubs. The Curfew Tower was built by Francis Turnley in 1817 to lock up any trouble makers in the village. It had a garrison of just one man, measures just 1.8 square metres in area, and is just over 12 metres in height. Turnley actually owned the village in the early nineteenth century and is responsible for developing it and the surrounding roads. With the table-topped Lurigethan Mountain overlooking Cushendall, this is truly one of the most picturesque villages in Northern Ireland.

Cushendall is also the start of a 40 kilometre section of the Causeway Coastal Route that almost exclusively runs by the seashore. It is no wonder that The Guardian newspaper named this route as one of the top five driving routes in the world in 2006. This road was built between 1832 and 1842 by William Bald, a Scottish engineer, who planned the road so that it ran around the edges of the coastal cliffs instead of running inland through more difficult terrain. He blasted the cliff faces and used the rubble on the shore to create the foundations for the new road. This was a fantastic engineering feat for the early nineteenth century and made a huge difference to the life of the people who lived here and in the Glens. Previously, locals sailed their goods the short distance across the North Channel to Scotland, as it was easier than travelling inland to trade.

Mural in Cushendall.

Just outside Cushendall I passed under the sandstone Red Arch on the way to the village of Waterfoot. The Arch is on a dangerous corner and it is not easy to stop to take a look. Just past the arch is a small

48

harbour where it is easier to stop and see the arch which was built by Francis Turnley. Overlooking the arch are the ruins of Red Bay Castle which was built in the early 1600s by the McDonnell clan, but was later destroyed by Cromwellian troops in 1652.

The village of Waterfoot lies at the end of the glen of Glenariff, and winds around the beach and sand dunes of Red Bay. The scenic Knockore Mountain with its steep cliffs, overlooked the village as I continued on southwards. On the southern side of Waterfoot there are the remains of a railway bridge called the White Arch. This was part of a railway that belonged to the Glenariff Iron Ore and Harbour Company which operated for only a few years after it opened 1873 before being closed. The railway line was just three feet (0.9 metres) narrow gauge, and was the first of its type in Ireland. There was once also a small pier close to the arch and the line ran for 6.4 kilometres from here to nearby mines in Glenariff. You can still see the embankment for the railway line on the land side of the road as you pass by.

The White Arch, Waterfoot.

Exploring Northern Ireland's Causeway and Mourne Coastal Routes

This part of the Causeway Coastal Route passes around what is known as Garron Point. The edge of Knockore Mountain continues cliff-like around the point leaving this wall of rock on one side and the sea on the other of the narrow road. While there are a few places to stop and admire the scenery, this is a road that needs your full attention as you ride or drive. At least you won't have to worry about dangerous animals crossing the road, some claim that the last wolf in Ireland was shot near here in 1712 (others claim that the last wolf was shot in County Carlow in 1786). Either way this was over a hundred years after wolves were wiped out in mainland Britain. Leaving Waterfoot there is a wonderful reminder that the Giro d'Italia passed through here with a pink painted fisherman and his bicycle sitting on the remains of an old concrete pier looking out to sea.

The Giro d'Italia comes to Waterfoot.

The town and village dotted coastline of Antrim continues south towards Carnlough with its picturesque white limestone wall surrounded harbour on the shoreline of Carnlough Bay. The limestone used to build the walls was taken from the nearby Gortin Quarry and two stone bridges were used to bring it to harbour by rail for export. The Carnlough Lime Company opened the railway in 1854. Today the railway line is used as a walkway to see the nearby local attraction of Cranny Waterfall. A stone pier was built here in the late eighteenth century to accommodate ships of up to twenty tonnes, but this was replaced in 1853 when the harbour that we see today was built to accommodate ships up to 300 tonnes to carry limestone for export. Carnlough's best known hotel, The Londonderry Arms, was built by a great-grandmother of Winston Churchill, Lady Frances Vane-Tempest. She was the Marchioness of Londonderry and was responsible for much of the early development of Carnlough as a village and harbour.

Carnlough Harbour.

Just 4 kilometres along the A2 from Carnlough is the village of Glenarm. It also marks the place where the southernmost of the nine Glens of Antrim reaches the sea. The village is named after this glen whose name means 'Valley of the Army'. Glenarm may also be one of the oldest villages in Ireland as it was granted a charter by King John in the thirteenth century. The village is located beside Glenarm Castle which is the family home of the Earls of Antrim. The current Earl, Alexander Randal Mark McDonnell, is the 9th Earl. The first Earl was

Exploring Northern Ireland's Causeway and Mourne Coastal Routes

Randal MacSorley MacDonnell who was awarded the title in 1620. He was also the fourth son of Sorley Boy McDonnell of Dunluce Castle.

Glenarm River beside Glenarm Castle.

Ballycastle to Larne

The castle and its walled gardens are open to the public during the summer and features a magnificent Barbican style gate and what is called the Conjuror's Tower. The tower was named after Captain Mark Kerr, who became the 5th Earl in 1855, he was regularly to be seen on top of the tower looking out to sea. After his death he became affectionately known as the 'Conjuror'.

I decided that even though my aim was to travel on coast roads as much as possible, that I would ride inland up the glen of Glenarm to Slemish Mountain. This was where Ireland's patron saint, Patrick, is thought to have lived from age 16 to 22. He had been captured in Britain by Irish pirates and enslaved as a shepherd on Slemish. According to legend he was so lonely on the mountain that he turned to prayer. In a vision he was encouraged to escape back to Britain where he became a priest. Later he returned to Ireland to convert the Irish to Christianity.

Slemish Mountain.

From Slemish Mountain St Patrick would have had an excellent view of the surrounding flat countryside. This type of hill is one of several hundred so-called 'Marilyns' in Ireland. These are hills with a prominence of over 150 metres in height. The name is a pun on another famous list of hills in Scotland called the 'Munros'. Slemish Mountain is the remains of a plug from an extinct volcano, one of over 30 such hills in Northern Ireland.

Back on the coast road I departed one of the oldest villages in Ireland and turned south towards Ballygally where one of the oldest occupied buildings in Ireland still stands. Ballygally Castle was built in 1625 and is now used as a hotel. It was built by Scotsman James Shaw who had come to Ireland in 1606 with his wife Isabella to seek his fortune. It is recognised as one of Ireland's best-preserved Scottish baronial style plantation houses. It was also a place of refuge for Protestants during the bitter mid-seventeenth century civil wars that gripped Britain and Ireland. Being so old it of course has a ghost! Isabella Shaw is said to haunt the castle by walking the corridors at night. Ballygally also has a popular beach which is bounded at the southern end by the prominent Ballygally Head. Out to sea I could see a lighthouse which is located on a series of rocks known as The Maidens or Hulin Rocks. It was built in 1829 alongside another tower which was also a lighthouse that was abandoned in 1903.

Ballygally Castle.

Chaine Memorial Tower, Larne.

The narrow road around Ballygally Head continues by the edge of the sea underneath towering volcanic rock formations. In the distance I got my first glimpse of the Islandmagee peninsula as I made my way towards my last stop in Larne on this section of the Causeway Coastal

Route. On the way I passed by one of the major attractions of the Route at Carnfunnock Country Park. It comprises of 191 hectares of woodland, gardens, and walking trails. The park attracts thousands of visitors each year who enjoy unique attractions like the Carnfunnock Maze which is a hedge shaped like a map of Northern Ireland.

The Friends Goodwill Memorial in Larne.

Ballycastle to Larne

The wonderful Antrim coast road that started in Waterfoot and runs along the edge of the sea ends as you enter the town of Larne. Having ridden my bike around the entire coast of Ireland I have to say that this is probably one of the best stretches of road that I had experienced. On a bike you get a great sense of closeness to the road, but this stretch also brings you close to the sea and the Antrim coastline at the same time.

Arriving in Larne I made my way towards the centre of the town when I spotted a sign for the 'Chaine Memorial Tower'. Curiosity got the better of me so I diverted towards the shore where this 27 metre high replica of an Irish round tower stands as a memorial to James Chaine. He was a linen manufacturer who played a huge part in the development of Larne Harbour in the mid nineteenth century. He was certainly an influential person who played a vital role in setting up a ferry service from Larne to Scotland and even a trans-Atlantic service between Larne, Glasgow, and New York. While the service to Scotland still exists today, the trans-Atlantic service ended in 1889 just a few years after his death at the early age of 44. He also promoted and financed railways from Larne to Ballymena. He lived in what became Carnfunnock Country Park, and represented Antrim as an MP in the Westminster Parliament. A plaque on the tower tells us that he was held in great 'esteem and affection' by the Larne community who built the tower in 1887 to his memory.

Larne is a busy harbour town with regular ferry services to Scotland and the Isle of Man. It has a long maritime history and strong links to emigration from Ireland to America since 1717 when the first migrants sailed from here to Boston. Emigration is commemorated with the fine 'Friends Goodwill' monument within Curran Park. It depicts a family from the first sailing from Larne to Boston on a ship called the 'Friends Goodwill'. It was the first of many ships to sail to America with mostly Ulster Presbyterians seeking religious freedom in the New World. Today Larne harbour is busy with up to 20 sailings a day coming in and out of the port. Just at the edge of the port are the ruins of Olderfleet Castle which is a thirteenth century tower house. Larne Lough was once called Olderfleet, and it was here that Edward Bruce, brother of Scottish King Robert the Bruce, landed with 6,000 soldiers in a failed attempt to conquer Ireland in 1315.

Exploring Northern Ireland's Causeway and Mourne Coastal Routes

I had come to the end of my second section of the Causeway Coastal Route. While it is a short section of the Route I had experienced great riding since leaving Ballycastle earlier in the day. By taking my time and stopping at each village and town along the way, this unique coast road has secured a place in my motorcyclist's heart.

Conjuror's Tower, Glenarm.

Larne to Belfast (40 kms)

The A2 road from Larne to Belfast winds its way around first Larne Lough, and then Belfast Lough. The road runs inland and for a while you cannot see the open sea as the Islandmagee Peninsula cuts off the view. The village of Glynn on the way features a small obelisk on its main street with the message 'All ye who pass by remember with gratitude the men of Glynn, Magheramorne, and Raloo who fell in the Great War 1914-1918'. As I pass by I am struck by this simple message on a simple war memorial, and think about how many others have 'passed by' this place in the hundred or so years since the First World War started.

Larne Lough.

Exploring Northern Ireland's Causeway and Mourne Coastal Routes

The Islandmagee Peninsula is a short detour from the Causeway Coastal Route. Despite its name, Islandmagee is not actually an island. There are several places of interest for the tourist to check out. The first of these is the Ballylumford Dolmen which is thought to be about 4,000 years old. It consists of four upright stones with a large stone across the top, but it is easy to miss as it is in the front garden of a private house on the Larne Lough side of the peninsula. At Ballylumford is Northern Ireland's largest electricity generating station with its three distinctive towers. This station generates about half of Northern Ireland's electricity, and also is connected to Scotland via the 64 kilometre long Moyle Interconnector.

On leaving Islandmagee and arriving at the entrance to Belfast Lough is the village of Whitehead. Unusually there are no streets with the suffix 'Street' in their name, though there are plenty with suffixes such as 'Road' or 'Avenue'. As a consequence, Whitehead is sometimes called 'The Town With No Streets'. The town is also on the railroad to Belfast and in the past was a popular seaside holiday destination for the people from the city. From the shore here you can see North County Down on the other side of Belfast Lough. For steam train enthusiasts, Whitehead is the location for Ireland's only remaining mainline steam engineering depot. This is where all locomotive and carriage maintenance is carried out. It is called Whitehead Excursion Station to distinguish it from the nearby regular station. The last mainline steam hauled passenger train in Ireland ran between Belfast and Whitehead in 1970.

Carrickfergus is the last town on the Causeway Coastal Route before it finishes in Belfast. The first inhabitant here was an Anglo-Norman knight called John de Courcy who arrived in Ireland in 1176. He built Carrickfergus Castle in 1178 and it has dominated the centre of the town ever since. It has the distinction of having been laid siege to by Scots, Irish, English, and French attackers. Edward Bruce was first to attack the castle in 1315 in a siege that lasted a year before the castle surrendered. Over the centuries the castle was attacked many times by local Irish chiefs, especially the powerful O'Neills. It also played a central role in the War of the Two Kings between forces loyal to James II who held the castle, and those loyal to William III. General Frederick Schomberg, William's commander in Ireland, besieged the castle for seven days before the garrison surrendered. The final attack was one of the most dramatic events in its history when Carrickfergus became briefly embroiled in the Seven Years War (1756-1763) between France and England. French troops under the command of Francois Thurot spent six days in Carrickfergus during which they ransacked the town and forced the castle's garrison to surrender for the last time.

Carrickfergus Castle.

On 14 June 1690, King William himself set foot in Ireland for the first time in Carrickfergus with over 6,000 troops to begin the campaign which led to the famed Battle of the Boyne. A fine statue of him erected in 1990 on the tercentenary of his landing here overlooks the harbour. Though he did not stay in Carrickfergus, he went straight to Belfast, he is fondly remembered here. Just a few years after he left, the last witchcraft trial ever held in Ireland took place in Carrickfergus in 1711. Eight women from nearby Islandmagee were convicted of bewitching 18-year old Mary Dunbar and were sentenced to a year in prison, plus four turns in the public stocks on market day.

King William III.

After a long day in the saddle I stayed in Carrickfergus for the night at the comfortable Dobbins Inn on High Street. There were plenty of places to choose from for my evening meal, in the end I selected the

Larne to Belfast

excellent PaPa Browns Grill. Carrickfergus is a very pleasant town to wander around, especially around the castle and along the promenade that starts at the castle and ends beside a small pier on the coast road known as Marine Highway. Across the road from the pier is an interesting and shiny sculpture of three medieval soldiers brandishing their swords and shields. I ended the evening watching the sun go down over Belfast Lough exhausted physically from the ride, and mentally from all the wonderful sights I had seen.

The Causeway Coastal Route comes to an end on the outskirts of Belfast at Whiteabbey. The route, including detours, is officially 314 kilometres (195 miles) long according to Discover Northern Ireland from Derry to Belfast. It took me three days to ride the route during which I comfortably saw and enjoyed the many places of interest. Of course, the more you stray off the route, the longer it is going to take. I travelled inland into Ballymoney, Armoy, and Slemish Mountain, but there are many other attractions tempting tourists away from the coast.

Between Whiteabbey and the first signs for the Mourne Coastal Route near Holywood in County Down lies the city of Belfast. A trip to Northern Ireland is not complete without spending a day in the second biggest city on the island of Ireland. The name Belfast comes from the Irish 'Béal Feirste', which means 'mouth of the sandy ford'. This is derived from the name of a local river - the Farset, which now runs under much of the city in a tunnel big enough to fit a bus. King James I granted a Royal Charter in 1613 giving Belfast 'town' status. It soon became a busy port for products such as wool and grain to be exported to and from Ireland. By the end of the seventeenth century other industries had also begun to develop in Belfast, including linen which, along with shipbuilding, was to make Belfast one of the most prosperous cities in the United Kingdom and Ireland. The city blossomed as an industrial hub during the eighteenth and nineteenth centuries. As a result of the Industrial Revolution, Belfast became the largest linen producing centre in the world, and for a time had a greater population than Dublin. In 1861, Edward Harland and Gustav Wolff set up a shipyard that for many years would be one of the greatest shipyards in the world. The famous and tragic *Titanic* was built here. The Harland and Wolff Company still exists today though it concentrates mostly on renewable energy products.

Exploring Northern Ireland's Causeway and Mourne Coastal Routes

The Obel Tower on the River Lagan.

As I rode towards the city centre I could see that Belfast is a renewed and vibrant city. The Obel Tower, which at 85 metres high is the tallest building in Ireland, dominates the Belfast skyline. I made straight for the city centre and first stopped at the tourist office in Donegall Square. Tourist offices are a good way to peruse all the literature about what to see and do in Belfast. I decided first to visit the nearby City Hall. In 1888, Queen Victoria gave Belfast the title of 'city', and it was decided that a new city hall would be built. The building was designed by Englishman Sir Alfred Brumwell Thomas, who won a public design competition, and is considered to be the finest example of Edwardian Baroque in Britain or Ireland. It took eight years to build and was opened on 1 August 1906, during a great time of prosperity for Belfast. The building is open to the public and I checked out the exhibition in The Boffin coffee shop where I learned that Belfast and Northern Ireland was home to many inventors such as John Boyd Dunlop (inventor of the inflatable tire), William Reid Clanny (inventor of the safety lamp for miners), Sir James Martin (inventor of the airplane ejector seat), William Thompson - later Lord Kelvin (inventor of the

Absolute Temperature Scale), Frank Pantridge (inventor of the portable defibrillator), and Thomas Andrews (inventor of liquid gas which we now use for coolant in refrigerators and fuel for rockets).

At the side of the City Hall is the Titanic Memorial Garden. A monument to the victims of the *Titanic* disaster was built in 1920 in Donegall Square, but was moved in 1959 into the grounds of the City Hall. It was renovated in 2012 for the centenary of the sinking of the *Titanic* on 15 April 1912 during its maiden voyage from Southampton to New York. 1,512 people lost their lives in the disaster and all their names are listed on fifteen bronze plaques in the Memorial Garden. I'm sure like thousands before me I looked up the list to see if there were any namesakes of mine listed on what is now known as 'The Belfast List'. To my surprise I found the name of Dr William Francis Norman O'Loughlin. It turns out that he was the Chief Surgeon on board the *Titanic* having spent over 40 years at sea. He was also the dean of the medical staff of the White Star Line, which owned the *Titanic*. Dr O'Loughlin was born in Tralee County Kerry, not far from where my own O'Loughlin grandparents were from. However, it is not known in our family if he is a relative of ours. Sadly, his body was never recovered after the disaster.

I had already decided that I would visit the Charles Lanyon designed Victorian gaol at Crumlin Road in North Belfast. This former gaol is where many Loyalist and Republican prisoners were imprisoned during 'The Troubles'. It was closed in 1996, but following restoration it is now one of Belfast's major tourist attractions. I joined a tour led by an ex-prisoner who regaled us with stories of crime and punishment in the prison since it received its first prisoner in 1846. It has housed such diverse prisoners as former First Minister of Northern Ireland, the Reverend Ian Paisley, and the former President of Ireland Éamon de Valera. Paisley spent six weeks in the prison in 1969 for organising an illegal demonstration, de Valera spent a month in solitary confinement in 1924 after illegally entering Northern Ireland.

The tour of the prison takes you down to the 'C Wing' where you can see the small cells where prisoners spent most of their days. Seventeen men were executed in Crumlin Road Gaol between 1854 and 1961. At the end of C wing is the death chamber where our tour guide described in macabre detail the last moments of the condemned prisoner before being hanged. Outside we were shown the spot in the gaol yard where fifteen of those executed are buried in unmarked graves. Two of those executed have been identified with DNA and reburied elsewhere by their families. One of these men was nineteen year old IRA man Tom Williams, who was hanged in 1942 for the murder of a policeman.

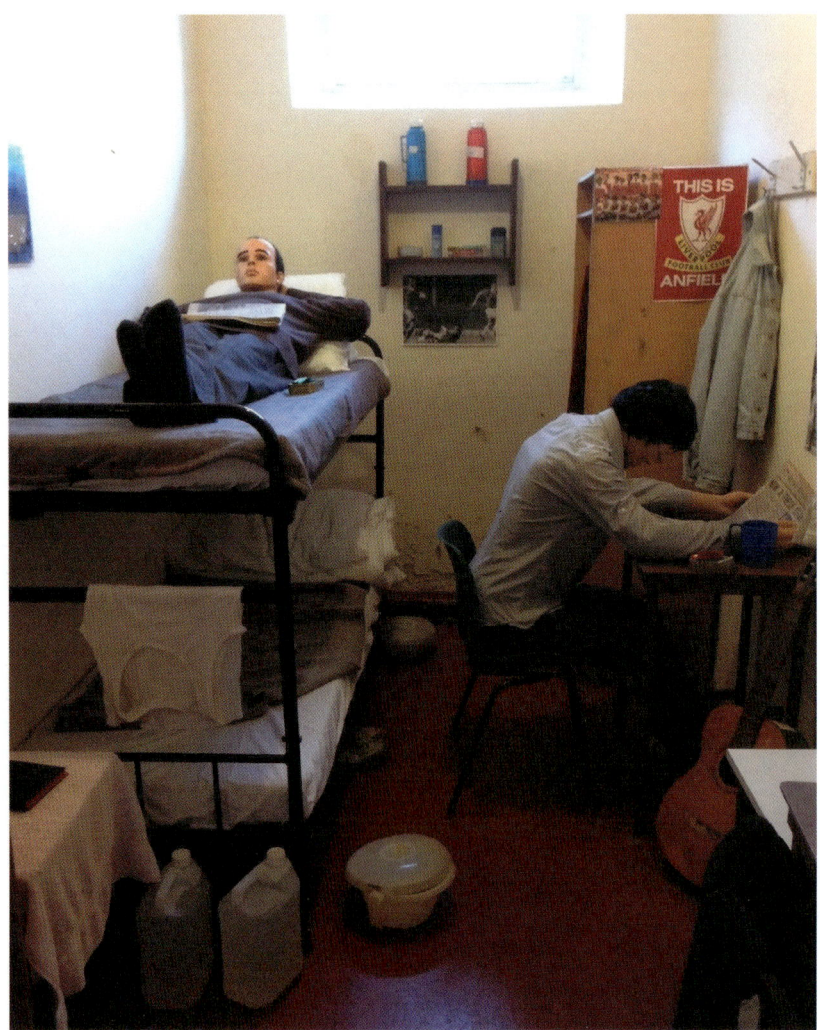

A cell in Crumlin Road Gaol.

The Titanic Experience.

My last stop in Belfast was at the Titanic Experience in the new Titanic Quarter which is one of the largest urban-waterfront regeneration projects in the world. Set in 185 acres of dockland, this is where the *Titanic* and its sister ships *Olympic* and *Britannic*, were built and launched between 1908 and 1914. The area is dominated by the shape of the Titanic Experience building which has four corners in the shape of the bow of the *Titanic*. It is well worth visiting the Titanic Experience, which won a UK Customer Experience Award in 2014, to see how the *Titanic* was built and learn much about this doomed ship which has been part of the heart of Belfast for over a century. You will see what the historic Harland and Wolff Drawing Offices looked like, with original drawings from the ships' designs all drawn by hand. My favourite part was the 'Shipyard Ride' which uses special effects and full-scale reconstructions to show us from the inside how ships were built in the early 1900s. Outside the building you can see the slipways where the *Titanic* was built and launched into Belfast Lough. You also can't miss the two huge yellow cranes, known as 'Samson' and 'Goliath',

Exploring Northern Ireland's Causeway and Mourne Coastal Routes

which are now iconic landmarks in Belfast. They were built in 1974 and 1969 respectively and are still in use today.

It was time to call it a day and settle down for the evening. I stayed at the excellent Fitzwilliam Hotel which is located beside the Grand Opera House which has entertained Belfast folk since 1895. It is a majestic building that bought applause and tears of laughter to all, but during The Troubles in the early 1970s it was almost demolished. It was saved after a campaign by the Ulster Architectural Society to have the building listed - the first building in Northern Ireland to be protected like this. The theatre was twice severely damaged by car bombs in the early 1990s, but this sturdy old building survived in true 'the show must go on' fashion. I settled for a quiet pint in Brennan's Bar, on what Belfast people call the 'Golden Mile', for the evening and relived the Causeway Coastal Route through the hundreds of photographs I had taken. It is with a heavy heart that I will leave Belfast behind tomorrow and all the wonderful attractions that this vibrant city has to offer. The few hours' duration of my visit does not in the least do it justice and I certainly recommend a stay of at least two or three days to see all the sights and experience everything Belfast has to offer.

Samson and Goliath cranes at the Harland & Wolff Shipyard.

Belfast to Portaferry (70 kms)

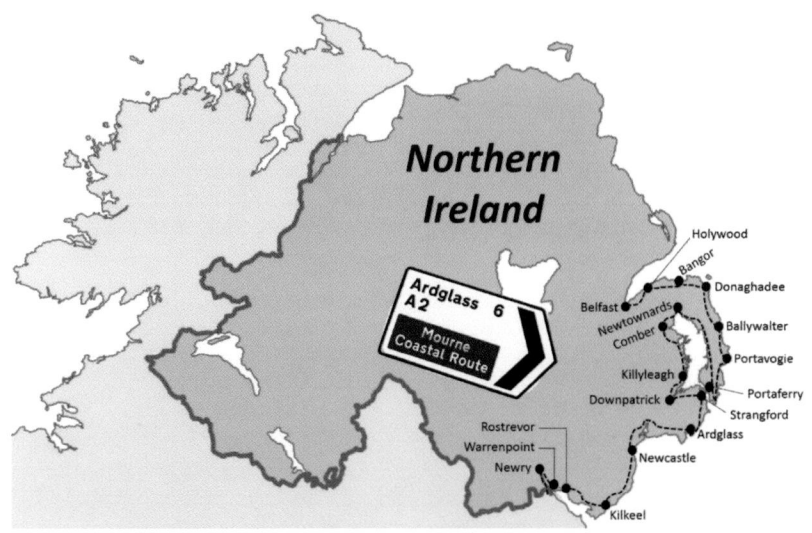

The Mourne Coastal Route.

The Mourne Coastal Route stretches from Belfast to Newry via the Ards Peninsula around the scenic Mountains of Mourne from which the route gets its name. It is almost exclusively based in County Down with just the very beginning at Belfast in County Antrim, and at the end where part of Newry is in County Armagh. Though not as well-known as the Causeway Coastal Route, this relatively newly created tourist route has just as much potential to fascinate. Starting in Belfast Lough it would take me and my bike along the North Channel between Ireland and Scotland and along the coast of the Irish Sea.

Leaving Belfast I was back on the A2 road as I started out across North County Down along the Sydenham By-Pass. The first landmark is the George Best Belfast City Airport, named in honour of Northern Ireland's greatest ever footballer who died in 2005 at the age of 59. The airport was first opened as 'Belfast Harbour Airport' in 1938 by Anne

Exploring Northern Ireland's Causeway and Mourne Coastal Routes

Chamberlain, wife of the then British Prime Minister Austin Chamberlain. As befitting Northern Ireland's strong links with Scotland, the first flight from the airport was to Glasgow. The A2 continues as a dual carriageway all the way to Bangor, but I was more interested in smaller coastal roads. At the town of Holywood I stopped briefly at The Esplanade to take one last look back at Belfast and south County Antrim which feels like it's just a few steps away across the Lough. Stopping briefly at The Dirty Duck Ale House for a coffee I studied my maps for the journey ahead in wonderful sunshine at this scenic spot.

The Holywood Esplanade overlooking Belfast Lough.

Holywood is regarded as the gateway to north County Down. It is a town with a rich and diverse heritage and dates back to a monastic settlement in the seventh century. In the nineteenth century the railway came to North Down and Holywood became the residence of choice for many of Belfast's wealthy industrial elite, who built great mansions here. Today, much of the town has been designated a conservation area. Holywood is also home to the only surviving Maypole in Ireland. It is located in the centre of the town and is still used every year during May Day celebrations. Holywood is known all over the world as home to golf superstar Rory McIlroy, winner of several golf majors. He learned his

Belfast to Portaferry

trade at the local Holywood Golf Club, though I'm sure he also played many times at the nearby Royal Belfast Golf Club which was founded in 1881 making it the oldest recognised golf club in Ireland.

Just outside Holywood on the Bangor road is the Ulster Folk & Transport Museum. The museum boasts a great collection of vintage vehicles including a 1960 yellow AA motorcycle and sidecar, a 1911 Minerva taxi, and two trams that once ran on the Giant's Causeway Tramway. The trams ran the 14.9 kilometres between Bushmills and Portrush via the Causeway from 1883 until the line was closed in 1949. The outdoor folk museum is set in 170 acres and shows us how the people of Ulster lived over 100 years ago. The 'village' of Ballycultra shows a variety of old buildings and houses which have been gathered from all around Ireland and rebuilt here as a typical Ulster village. The museum is also home to much of Ireland's archival material with photographic, audio, video, and folk heritage being carefully restored and archived here. The Ulster Folk & Transport Museum is a fantastic family day out and I recommend setting aside a few hours to see as much as you can. After my brief stop it was time to hit the road again.

The old and the new at the Ulster Folk & Transport Museum.

Main Street, Crawfordsburn.

    The picturesque village of Crawfordsburn lies just over one kilometre from the edge of Bangor, North Down's largest town. The village has a quaint black and white look and feel to it. At the centre of the village is the 'Old Inn' part of which has a distinctive thatched roof. This is the oldest part of the Inn that dates from the very early 1600s at the time of the end of the reign of Queen Elizabeth I. Records show that this building has existed in its present form since 1614.

Eisenhower Pier in Bangor Harbour.

Bangor is a busy bustling seaside resort that due to its proximity to Belfast is very much a commuter town for its bigger neighbour. This is a very old town that is thought to date back to as early as the mid-sixth century when a monastery was created here. With at one time over 3,000 monks in the monastery, it was well-known as a seat of learning from which missionaries were sent to all over Europe. The modern Bangor Abbey is situated on the site where previous churches were built and destroyed by Vikings. It was restored in the twelfth century by St Malachy who was the Abbot - some of his work remains today in the form of St Malachy's Wall. A plaque on the wall shows how the Abbey might have looked based on a 1625 map by Thomas Raven. The church's cemetery has several interesting gravestones including a memorial to the Assistant Surgeon on the Titanic, Dr John Simpson from Bangor. He would of course have assisted the Chief Surgeon

William O'Loughlin during the Titanic's ill-fated voyage, in which he also perished.

I made my way down to the town's harbour where I parked beside the old Harbour Master's Office across the street from the Old Custom House. The Office was built around 1860, but is no longer used by the harbour master. In the past it has served as both an RNLI lifeboat station, and a restaurant. The Custom House, featuring a fine round tower, was built in 1637 by James Hamilton who was from Scotland. This building is now a Tourist Information Office where I searched in vain for information about the Mourne Coastal Route. Hamilton arrived in Bangor having been given lands by King James I, and modern Bangor dates from this time. The main pier here is called Eisenhower Pier after the 34th President of the United States, Dwight D. Eisenhower. It was here that 'Ike' made a historic send-off on 19 May 1944, to hundreds of Allied warships gathered in Bangor before the D-Day Normandy Invasion of Europe. Warships like the USS Arkansas, USS Texas, and USS Nevada were based in Belfast Lough, and following Ike's speech on board the USS Quincy, the convoy of ships sailed down the Irish Sea, around the coast of England and across the Channel. A plaque on the pier commemorates the occasion and it was erected to commemorate the 70th anniversary of the D-Day landings when Mary-Jean Eisenhower, grand-daughter of the former President, officially renamed the pier in his honour. It is also worth walking out to the end of the pier to see five mosaics which depict Bangor's role during World War II.

Continuing along the A2, I stopped at the seaside village of Groomsport. It is believed that it was from here that the first ship to set sail from Ulster to America departed. In 1636, just 16 years after the Pilgrim Fathers landed at Plymouth Rock in Pennsylvania after crossing the Atlantic on the *Mayflower*, the *Eagle Wing* set sail with about 140 Presbyterians on board but had to turn back following a storm in the mid-Atlantic. This event is celebrated every July with the Eagle Wing 3-day Festival. The small harbour, reputed to be of Viking origin, is today home to pleasure boats and small fishing vessels. Also on the water front are the restored Cockle Row Cottages. These cottages show what life was like for a fisherman and his family at the beginning of the twentieth century, and also house a Visitor Information Centre.

One of the many ruins of windmills on the Ards Peninsula.
This one is in Portaferry.

As I returned to the A2 the road starts to wind its way southwards and the tiny Copeland Islands come into view. These are a set of three islands; Mew Island, Lighthouse Island, and the larger Copeland Island. Though uninhabited now, at one time up to 100 people lived on these islands surviving through farming and fishing. The closest town to the Copeland Islands is Donaghadee where many of the islands' inhabitants traded their produce for cash. Donaghadee stretches out northwards along the coast with houses lining the coast road for quite a distance before you reach the centre of the town. This is the nearest port in Ireland to Scotland and the harbour here was once the main point of landing for people travelling from Britain to Ulster. In its heyday in 1812, during the Napoleonic Wars, over 20,000 cattle and horses were exported to Portpatrick just 34 kilometres away across the North Channel. Portpatrick was also a destination for young people who travelled from Donaghadee to get a quick marriage with no questions asked - giving it the name 'Gretna Green for Ireland'.

About 5 kilometres south of Donaghadee is the village of Millisle. This is home to the only remaining working windmill on the Ards Peninsula which is called the Ballycopeland Windmill. It was built in the late eighteenth century and continued in use until the First World War. It is now restored and in working order. At one time over 50 windmills dotted the landscape of the peninsula. Most were built by local landowners and at one time the peninsula was known as 'Little Holland'. Many of the ruins of these windmills are still in existence and can be seen on the mostly flat landscape of this part of the Mourne Coastal Route.

The Ards Peninsula is a popular seaside holiday destination with many caravan and mobile home parks dotted along the coast road. The biggest of these is the Ballyferris Holiday Park, part of which juts magnificently out to the sea, which is close to the quiet village of Ballywalter. The coast here has lots of sandy beaches and on a clear day you can see both Scotland and the Isle of Man. The peninsula is also popular with cyclists with a ride up and down making a nice 75 kilometre spin on mostly flat roads. The village of Ballyhalbert lies about half way down the peninsula and is close to the most easterly part of the island of Ireland at Burr Point. This makes for a nice quartet of land marks for me in that I have been to the most northerly (Malin Head in County Donegal), southerly (Mizen Head in County Cork), westerly (Dunmore Head in County Kerry), and now the most easterly point in Ireland at Burr Point in County Down on my bike. Ballyhalbert also played a key

Belfast to Portaferry

role during the Second World War when it was home to a Royal Air Force base. It protected the shipyards in Belfast from German air raids, and was once visited by General Dwight D. Eisenhower in on 14 May 1944 - just 24 days before the D-Day Normandy landings.

Not far from Ballyhalbert is the most eastern settlement in Ireland at the fishing village of Portavogie. I rode down to the harbour where fish are landed that end up on many restaurant menus in Northern Ireland. Portavogie is famous for its herrings and prawns, which have given rise to a fish processing industry as well as boat building in the harbour. In the harbour there is a poignant sculpture in memory of local fishermen who were 'lost or died at sea' - many with the same surname. Portavogie is also home to one of Ireland's best known sporting venues at Kirkistown Motor Racing Circuit which is just 1 kilometre inland from the village. The circuit was built on an old war time airfield and has been home to the 500 Motor Racing Club of Ireland since 1953. The club's name is inspired from the then new 500cc Formula 3 for small single seat racing cars which were powered by motorcycle engines. Several Irish motorsport stars such as Joey Dunlop, Martin Donnelly, and Eddie Irvine raced at Kirkistown before going on to further their careers elsewhere.

Further along the Ards Peninsula is the picturesque village of Cloughey. Its most famous landmark is Kirkistown Castle which was built by Roland Savage in 1622 following the Ulster Plantation. It is not a castle in the accepted sense, but is rather a tower house of the type common in Ireland in the seventeenth century. It resembles the gatehouse of a Norman castle and is surrounded by a fortified enclosure with towers on each corner. Cloughey is also close to one of the most dangerous stretches of coastline in Ireland where the North and South Rocks lie some distance out to sea. A lifeboat station was established in Cloughey in 1884 following the events of the previous year when disaster was averted after a tea clipper, the 'Wild Deer', ran aground on the North Rock. There were 300 emigrants and 40 crew on board travelling from Glasgow to New Zealand - all survived.

The ride down through the east side of the Ards Peninsula is through narrow roads edged with neat hedges and wonderful views out to sea. Just south of Cloughey is the tiny village of Kearney. This is an old village carefully restored by the National Trust as an authentic traditional fishing village. The Trust owns many of the cottages, though they are not open to the public. During the nineteenth century this was a bustling fishing location which had the distinction of having a fishing boat crewed entirely by women called the 'she-cruiser' for fishing in the local waters. Just past Kearney is Ballyquintin Castle which is one of the few Norman castles left in Ireland that is still inhabited. It is private and not open to the public, it can only be seen at a distance from the road.

Kirkistown Castle, Cloughey.

The southernmost part of the Ards Peninsula is at Ballyquintin Point. This also marks the point where the North Channel between Ireland and the Mull of Galloway in Scotland ends, and the Irish Sea begins. There are wonderful views of the Mourne Mountains in the distance from Barr Hall bay, which also marks the entrance to Strangford Lough. This lough is one of only three Marine Nature Reserves in the UK, and it is also a designated Area of Outstanding Beauty as well as an Area of Special Scientific Interest. The name 'Strangford' is derived from old Norse words meaning 'strong fiord'. The entrance to the lough is called The Narrows where at spring tide the speed of the waters coming into or out of the lough can reach 7.8 knots

Belfast to Portaferry

(14.45 kilometres per hour), with 350 million tonnes of water flowing through The Narrows with each tide. This is one of the fastest tides in the world and it is no wonder that The Narrows now features the world's first commercial scale tidal device built by SeaGen in 2008. This tidal turbine can generate over 8GWh of electricity, and has been instrumental in research to harness the power of the sea.

The road from Barr Hall northwards runs right alongside the lough to the town of Portaferry. Here the Mourne Coastal Route runs across the lough by ferry to the town of Strangford on the other side, and I had to make a decision as to whether I would take the ferry or go the long way around to Strangford. On a pleasant sunny afternoon it was an easy decision to make, and I set off on the 85 kilometre round trip around Strangford Lough.

Portaferry to Strangford (85 km)

Strangford Lough is the largest sea lough in Ireland or the UK - it is also a Marine Nature Reserve. It includes several areas of special interest to marine conservationists and is recognised internationally as a major location for marine research. Arriving in Portaferry I first make my way to Windmill Hill overlooking the town. From here is one of the best viewing points in the lower part of the Ards Peninsula - you can see southwards towards the Irish Sea and the Mourne Mountains, west towards the town of Strangford, east towards the Isle of Man, and northwards up though Strangford Lough over the town of Portaferry.

View northwards over Portaferry to Strangford Lough.

Portaferry to Strangford

At the top of Windmill Hill are the remains of Tullyboard Windmill that are still in good condition. It was one of the many windmills that dotted the hills of the Ards Peninsula and was built in 1771. Like other windmills in this area it was used for scutching flax and for grinding grain. However, it was destroyed by a fire on Christmas Day in 1878. From the top of Windmill Hill you can see the old St Patrick's Church, which was built in 1762, and its adjoining cemetery. I pay a visit to the grave of my dear Aunt Breda who is also my Godmother. On a bright sunny afternoon looking out over Strangford Lough, this seemed like the most beautiful and peaceful resting place in Ireland.

Portaferry is well known as a boarding point for the short ferry journey across the lough to Strangford. Watch out for the ferry going sideways when the tide is in full flow. Overlooking the small harbour where the ferry arrives and departs is Portaferry Castle. On the seaward side the castle is intact, but several walls have fallen on the landward side. It was built in the sixteenth century by William Le Savage, who was a descendant of the 'Savages of Ards'. This family were Norman knights who invaded England with William the Conqueror and came to Ulster in 1177 to seek their fortune. You can go inside to look at the thick walls and see the places where wooden floors once crossed overhead. Beside the castle is the Exploris Aquarium, which is well worth a visit to see the fascinating marine life from the lough and from the Irish Sea. Also here is the Portaferry Lifeboat Station which replaced the Cloughey station in 1980. One of its best known rescues was on 26 May 1985 when a converted fishing vessel, the 'Tornamona', hit rocks and sank at the entrance to Strangford Lough. On board were the Dunlop brothers, Joey and Robert, who were on their way from Portaferry to the Isle of Man TT races with a cargo of racing bikes.

Leaving Portaferry I start my journey around Strangford Lough riding northwards with the lough on my left and the drumlin landscape on my right. At Kircubbin I stop for petrol and meet with a fellow Harley-Davidson rider who told me about the strong links between motorcycling and the Ards peninsula. Kircubbin was once a busy harbour taking advantage of deep waters in the sheltered lough. It was a busy centre for trade in the nineteenth century for local production of linen, embroidery, soda ash (made from sea kelp), and even straw hats and bonnets. A short ride away from Kircubbin is the village of Greyabbey, which gets its name from the nearby ruined Cistercian monastery built in 1193. Legend has it that when the monks of the abbey felt the need of female company they would turn themselves into crows and fly over the abbey wall into the village to pick up unsuspecting women, and bring them back to the abbey for some fun. The village of Greyabbey is noted for featuring several antique shops and the nearby Mount Stewart House and Gardens. The garden here is one of the finest in Ireland with a rich diversity of plants to explore. The house was built in the late eighteenth and early nineteenth centuries by the Stewart family who hold the title of Marquis of Londonderry. One of the Stewart family who lived in Mount Stewart was Robert, the second Marquis. He was better known as Viscount Castlereagh and he served as Chief Secretary of Ireland during the 1798 Rebellion, and later as British Foreign Secretary during the Napoleonic Wars. The house is open to the public and features a fine collection of Stewart family memorabilia and valuables. Just off the coast of Greyabbey is one of the largest uninhabited islands in Strangford Lough - Chapel Island. It can be accessed on foot across the mud flats during low tide and was a place of prayer and meditation for the monks from Greyabbey.

At the northern end of Strangford Lough is the town of Newtownards. All along the coast road on the way into Newtownards you can see a tower on a hill overlooking the town. This is the 41 metre high Scrabo Tower which was erected in memory of Charles William Vane, the third Marquis of Londonderry in 1857. He was a half-brother to Viscount Castlereagh and was known as 'Fighting Charlie' during the Napoleonic Wars. He fought with the Duke of Wellington in the Peninsular Campaign and distinguished himself at the battles of Busaco and Talavera. Scrabo Hill is all that's left of an extinct volcano, and is also the location for the Scrabo Golf Club. The tower is open to the public during the summer months and you can climb the 122 steps to the top for some of the best views in County Down.

Newtownards is a bustling town and I parked the bike in the town centre at Conway Square for a look around. The square is busy with people enjoying the sun and moving about with full shopping bags. I notice a statue in front of the Town Hall and I was intrigued to discover that it was a memorial to Lt Col Blair "Paddy" Mayne (1915 - 1955), who was the founder of the Special Air Service (SAS) during World War II. As well as being a soldier he was also solicitor, an amateur boxer, and he played rugby for Ireland and the British & Irish Lions in a tour of

South Africa. Mayne was born and grew up in Newtownards, and came back to practice as a solicitor after the war.

Scrabo Tower.

Just north of Newtownards is the Somme Heritage Centre which was opened in 1994. It examines the roles of the 10th, 16th, and 36th volunteer Irish Divisions that took part in World War I. On the first day of the Battle of the Somme on 1 July 1916, the 36th (Ulster) Division suffered over 4,900 casualties, with 79 officers and 1,777 other ranks killed. Memories go deep here and it is fitting that such slaughter and sacrifice be respectfully commemorated for future generations.

It was time to turn south again and I left Newtownards to ride down the western side of Strangford Lough. Unlike the eastern side where the road runs right along the coast, the western side is a series of narrow roads that run close to, but not on the edge of the lough. An 8 kilometre dual carriageway takes you all the way from Newtownards to Comber and it is a pleasant, if short lived, experience to open up the throttle on the bike after so many narrow roads since leaving Derry four days ago. In the town centre there is a brilliant column with a statue of Major General Rollo Gillespie, a soldier who was born in Comber in 1766. Gillespie was killed at the Battle of Kalunga in far-away Nepal in 1814. This 16.5 metre high monument in the only public Masonic monument in Ireland. His last words were: 'One shot more for the honour of Down'. The town also has a link to the Titanic as it was here that the man with overall responsibility for building the ship, Thomas Andrews, was born in 1873. He died on Titanic's maiden voyage.

Sketrick Castle, Strangford Lough.

Portaferry to Strangford

The twisty roads south are a pleasure to ride amidst the very green pastures of the countryside. While the roads are narrow and command full attention, the calm waters of Strangford Lough are never far away. The lough is a popular place for boating and the Down Cruising Club shows its love of the sea by using the Light Vessel (L.V.) Petrel as its clubhouse in Ballydorn Bay. The Petrel was built in Dublin in 1915 as a lightship, all Irish light vessels were named after sea birds at that time. Most of her service life was at Blackwater Bank on the River Blackwater in Co Wexford, but since 1968 she has served as an iconic clubhouse for local sailors. Close by are the ruins of the twelfth century Sketrick Castle across a short causeway on Sketrick Island. It was owned by one of the 'Savages of Ards' – Sir Robert Savage, and it was intact until as recently as 1896 when most of the tower house shaped building was destroyed in a storm.

In this western part of the middle of Strangford Lough there are many small islands. These are in fact what are called 'drowned drumlins', part of a chain of thousands of small tightly packed hills which run across Ireland from County Down to County Donegal. These small hills are usually about 300 metres long and 100 metres wide and were made by glaciers during the Ice Age 20,000 years ago when most of Ireland was covered in ice. The ride south along narrow winding roads towards the town of Killyleagh is dotted with drumlins both on land and in the lough. When humans first started to populate areas like this after the ice age they realised the safety potential of drumlins as the built 'raths' or small forts on top of these hills. Approaching the hilly town of Killyleagh I spotted the large castle which overlooks the town from a high vantage point. Parts of the castle date back to 1180 and it was re-designed by Sir Charles Lanyon in the mid nineteenth century. It is believed to be one of the oldest inhabited castles in Ireland. The Hamilton family have lived here since the early seventeenth century, and the castle is therefore not open to the public. In 1649 forces loyal to Oliver Cromwell sailed up Strangford Lough and bombarded the castle. It was repaired in 1666 by Henry Hamilton who also built the huge gate at the entrance to the castle. There is also a war memorial to the right of the gate house dedicated to 'the men of Killyleagh who gave their lives for others in the great war, 1914-1918'. The memorial was decorated with poppy wreaths and I read the lines at the bottom of the list of names of those who died, which I later discovered are a variation of lines from the hymn 'O Valiant Hearts', written by Englishman Sir John Stanhope Arkwright in honour of the dead in World War I: "*Splendid they passed, The great surrender made, Into that light, That never more shall fade.*

The gatehouse at Killyleagh Castle.

Portaferry to Strangford

Leaving Killyleagh I ride towards Downpatrick, which as its name suggest, has strong links with Saint Patrick. The name comes from the Irish *Dún Pádraig*, which means 'Patrick's Fort'. It is at Down Cathedral where Saint Patrick is reputed to be buried along with the other patron saints of Ireland; Saint Brigid and Saint Columba. Downpatrick is also located on the 148 kilometre Saint Patrick's Trail which runs from Bangor to Armagh. As I saw earlier, Patrick had been a slave on Slemish Mountain. After he escaped he made his way back to Britain where studied in a monastery to become a bishop. In the year 432 he came back to Ireland to convert the Irish to Christianity, and landed close to Downpatrick in Strangford Lough. He died in 461 and was buried here on the site where the cathedral stands today. Nearby the cathedral is the Saint Patrick Centre which is the only permanent exhibition in the world about Patrick.

St Patrick's grave at Down Cathedral.

Downpatrick is one of Ireland's most ancient and historic towns. It is believed that there were settlements here as long ago as the year 130, and it was given the name *Dún Pádraig* in the thirteenth century which later was anglicized to Downpatrick. The Down County Museum located in the town near the Cathedral tells of 9,000 years of history in the area. The museum was once a Gaol which was opened in 1796 just in time for the 1798 Rebellion. There were only 18 small cells that at times accommodated up to 130 prisoners in dreadful conditions. When a new gaol was built in 1830, it became a barracks for the South Down Militia. During World War II Canadian and American troops were stationed here, but the barracks fell into disrepair in the 1970s. In 1980 it was purchased by Down County Council to restore as the museum we see today. The gaol's most famous prisoner was United Irishman Thomas Russell. Originally from County Cork, Russell was hanged outside Downpatrick Goal on 21 October 1803 for his part in the rebellion by Robert Emmett in Dublin that same year. He is immortalized as 'the man from God knows where' in a ballad written by Bangor woman Florence Mary Wilson. Many convicts were transported from Downpatrick Gaol to the penal colony of New South Wales in Australia. The gaol has a database of the 400 convicts who were transported – the first name listed is that of Anne Atcheson who was sentenced to seven years transportation on 14 August 1827 for 'Stealing Fowls'. She was one of 66 women transported from here, most of whom were convicted of petty crimes such as stealing clothes and shoplifting.

After spending a couple of hours experiencing the historic sights of Downpatrick I pointed the bike eastwards from the town towards Strangford. On the way near the village of Saul I crossed over the tiny Slaney River which enters Strangford Lough at the site where Saint Patrick landed on his return to Ireland. From here he made his way to the village of Saul where the local chieftain, called Dichu, was his first convert to Christianity. There is another reminder of Saint Patrick near the village of Raholp where there are the ruins of Saint Tassach's Church, which dates from the tenth century. Saint Tassach was Bishop of Raholp and is most well-known for giving the Last Rights to Saint Patrick as he lay dying.

The best known attraction on the way to the village of Strangford is Castle Ward, an eighteenth century building and park that is now managed by the National Trust. It is open to the public and is set in 820 acres of gardens. The main house is very unusual in that the front and the back are in different architectural styles. It was built in the early 1760s for Bernard Ward, who later became Lord Bangor, and his wife

Portaferry to Strangford

Lady Ann Magill. However, they disagreed on the style that the house should be built to – they could not agree whether they would build to a Classic Palladian or Gothic styles. So they split their differences – literally. The south-west façade is in classic style, while the north-east is gothic. Even inside the house the differences between husband and wife continued with a divide down the centre of the building. The grounds of the Castle Ward were used recently in the Game of Thrones TV series as the location of Winterfell, and you can take part in archery shooting as part of the Game of Thrones experience.

The Classical Palladian façade, Castle Ward.

I reached the end of my detour around Strangford Lough at the village of the same name. It is directly across the lough from Portaferry and is a picturesque village with nineteenth century houses on the waterfront facing the lough. The village is centred around the small harbour with the ferry facilities taking centre stage. Also in the centre of the village is a sixteenth century tower house called Strangford Castle. Its walls are over one metre think and it is about ten metres high. Look closely at the top of the walls to see crenellations, which are spaces along the top of the wall, through which arrows could have been shot. You can also see gun loops which are round holes in the walls for defending the castle.

The town of Portaferry viewed from Strangford harbour.

The 85 kilometre detour from the Mourne Coastal Route is definitely worth taking as there is so much to see and do around Strangford Lough. You'll need at least half a day to enjoy the wide variety of sights, but for me it was now time to ride southwards along the Irish Sea and the remainder of the County Down coast.

Strangford to Newcastle (45 kms)

Leaving Strangford I am back on the A2 road that that I started on outside Derry a few days ago. For the first part of the journey the road runs along the shore to the tiny village of Kilclief, and it is with fond memories that I say goodbye to Strangford Lough. Here you can't miss the well preserved Kilclief tower house at the side of the road. It is a great example of the type of fortified houses built by local landlords in the early fifteenth century. An Environment and Heritage Service sign at the gate to the castle contains a diagram to show how the inside of the castle would have looked when it was inhabited. It was built by John Sely who was Bishop of Down, but he was evicted from the castle and deprived if his bishopric because of a relationship with a married woman by none other than Pope Eugene IV. There is another Eugene connection to Kilclief in that two disciples of St Patrick, brothers Neill and Eugenius, were partly responsible for the first church that was built here.

Directly opposite Kilclief Castle is a short detour from the A2 that takes you through Killard Nature Reserve. This is a popular location for walkers who like to explore the rugged coastline of Killard Point which marks the southern end of Strangford Lough. The reserve has been used in the past as a hurling pitch and a temporary RAF radar station. The effects of the last Ice Age can be seen here as moving glaciers smoothed the rocks on the shore. Just past the Reserve you can see the uninhabited Guns Island which lies off the coast near the village of Ballyhornan. This is also home to the Cable Bar which is named after a telecommunications cable that runs from Ballyhornan to the Isle of Man.

I next stopped in Ardglass, a beautiful harbour village which is known for being home to four medieval tower houses – the most of any village in Ireland. The most impressive is Jordan's Castle, named after a certain Simon Jordan who defended the castle for three years from the O'Neills during the Nine Year's War until relieved in 1601. The castle is not open to the public, but you can walk right around it and admire its imposing height.

Jordan's Castle, Ardglass.

Just outside Ardglass I noticed a sign for Coney Island. This is one of three 'islands' in Ireland with this name – one other is near Strandhill in County Sligo, while the third is at the southwest corner of Lough

Strangford to Newcastle

Neagh in County Armagh. The original name in Irish means 'the island of rabbits', and is one of several possible sources for the name given to Coney Island in New York. Here the name relates to a row of houses leading out to a small hill. This Coney Island is also made famous by Van Morrison who wrote a song called 'Coney Island'. Written in 1989, the Coney Island mentioned in the song is the final destination of a road trip taken by Morrison that started out from Downpatrick.

Coney Island, Ardglass.

The village of Killough lies across a small bay from Coney Island and is a joy to ride through as its main street is lined with sycamore trees. The village was previously known as St Anne's Port, and was once one of County Down's busiest ports exporting grain during the early nineteenth century. Just past Killough is Dundrum Bay with its spectacular back drop of the Mourne Mountains. From here you get a real appreciation of the famous line from the song written about these mountains by Percy French in 1896: 'Where the Mountains of Mourne Sweep Down to the Sea'. Dundrum Bay is also known for its seal sanctuary at Minerstown at the eastern side of the bay. There were no seals on display for me to see, but I did discover from an Action for Biodiversity sign at the sanctuary that seals make themselves into a banana shape when on high alert – viewers are warned to stay away if a seal is 'banana-ing'.

Dundrum Bay gets its name from the village of Dundrum which you have to pass through inland as you travel around the bay. It is best known for the ruins of an early thirteenth century Norman castle. England's King John visited here in 1210 as this castle was an important fortress protecting the local coastline and the road to Downpatrick. It started to fall into ruin after the English Civil War in the mid seventeenth century. Though you can't see it from the roads as you pass by, a fine sandy beach runs along much of Dundrum Bay. Bordering the bay is Ireland's first Nature Reserve at Murlough where some of the sand dunes have been dated as being over 6,000 years old and are amongst the highest dunes in Europe. Also here is the Royal County Down Golf Club where the Irish Open was played in 2015. In the mid nineteenth century Dundrum Bay made headlines all over the world when the then longest passenger ship in the world, the ss Great Britain, was stranded in the bay for nearly a year. The metal ship, designed by Isambard Brunel, crashed into the bay as a result of a huge navigational error that did not take into account the effect that a metal hull would have on a magnetic compass. The ship became a major salvage operation that at the time was regarded as the birth of modern ship salvaging methods. After refloating, it was used primarily for shipping between Britain and Australia. The ss Great Britain is now a major visitor attraction in Bristol Harbour.

At the foot of the eastern side of the Mourne Mountains is the town of Newcastle. The highest mountain in Northern Ireland, Slieve Donard, dominates the town. It is named after St Domangart who was a sixth century holy man who is reputed to have built a prayer cell on top of the mountain. All the hills and mountains here are nearly covered in trees – this has to be one of the most scenic locations on the Mourne Coastal Route. In the busy town there is a promenade along the shore that features a memorial fountain to Percy French, but all the time it feels as if you are just a few steps away from sweeping up to the mountains. Slieve Donard can be climbed quite easily as there is a path all the way to the top. On a clear day you can see as far north as Belfast, and as far south as Dublin. Also of interest here in the mountains is the

Strangford to Newcastle

35 kilometre granite Mourne Wall. It was built between 1904 and 1922 to enclose the water catchment area of the Mourne Mountains, and it is regularly used as a marker by hill walkers.

Slieve Donard overlooking Newcastle.

Newcastle is an old town thought to date back as far as 1433, and like many of the towns and villages along the County Down coast became an important fishing port. Tragedy stuck in 1843 when fourteen local fishing boats were lost in a storm and 46 men from Newcastle perished. The area is also known for Mourne granite which was once quarried and exported from Newcastle to make paving stones in New York and London. Some Mourne granite has also been used to form part of the base of the 9/11 Memorial in New York. Today as I parked my bike beside the promenade and went for a stroll I absorbed the beauty and history of this seaside resort – a jewel on the Mourne Coastal Route.

Kilclief Castle.

Newcastle to Newry (62 kms)

The last section of my motorcycle odyssey around Northern Ireland swings around the southern side of the Mourne Mountains and right around Carlingford Lough. Slieve Donard and the rest of the Mourne Mountains will be at my side for next hour of wonderful riding. While the mountains look imposing, it is quite a small range that is just over ten kilometres wide. Just like in County Antrim the road hugs the beautiful coastline for long distances, and all the time I wanted to slow down to absorb the scenery properly.

Not far outside Newcastle on the Kilkeel Road a sign greets you to the 'Kingdom of Mourne'. This was a small ancient 'kingdom' enclosed by the Mourne Mountains which was cut off from the rest of Ireland for centuries due to the difficult approaches by land. Without any roads, access to this region was by either on foot or by the sea. The area gives rise to a lot of tales, myths, and legends. It was from these mountains near here that St Patrick is reputed to have banished all the snakes from Ireland. There is also the wonderfully named 'Maggie's Leap' – this is a wide chasm in the cliff face that is best viewed from the sea. It got its name from a local poacher's daughter called Maggie who escaped from soldiers by leaping over the chasm. Just past Maggie's Leap is a small car park located in an area known as the 'Bloody Bridge'. It is not certain where this name came from but it is thought to most likely refer to a massacre that occurred here during the 1641 Rebellion. It is not known how many people were killed, but their bodies were reputedly thrown over the bridge into the river below making it run red with blood.

The first village I reached on this section of the Mourne Coastal route was Annalong. Like many of the towns and villages in Northern Ireland during July, the main street was decorated with colourful red, white, and blue flags and bunting. The Orange Arch beside the Presbyterian Church commemorates both the Battle of the Boyne in 1690, and the Battle of the Somme in 1916. Annalong is home to one of the last working watermills in Ireland. It was built in the early nineteenth century and milled corn until the 1960s. It is located near the mouth of the Annalong River which powered its large water wheel. The mill was restored and reopened as a visitor attraction in 1985. In it you will see a heritage display that gives us an insight into life in Annalong long ago. The harbour here was also a place of export for Mourne granite, though today it is home to small fishing boats and cruisers.

Orange Arch in Annalong.

The town of Kilkeel was once the 'capital' of the Kingdom of Mourne. It gets its name from the fourteenth century church ruins overlooking the town. In Irish, the name was 'Cill Chaoil' meaning Church of the Narrows. There has been a settlement here since the eleventh century and today Kilkeel has one of the largest fishing fleets in Ireland. The large harbour hosts the fishing fleet and many other boats. The Mourne Maritime Visitor Centre documents Kilkeel's fishing and maritime heritage. In May 1918 a German U-Boat sank five boats from the Kilkeel fleet. The U-Boat surfaced in the middle of the fleet while they were fishing for herring off the coast at Kilkeel. The German captain ordered all the fishermen off the boats into small punts, and then sank the boats by placing a bomb in each. It is reported that the

Germans shared their gin and cigarettes with the fishermen who were then allowed to row ashore and no lives were lost. One person of historical note that did die in Kilkeel was William Hare, one half of the infamous Burke & Hare murderers who committed sixteen murders in Edinburgh between 1827 and 1828. Hare turned King's evidence to testify against Burke who was hanged for the crimes. Hare left Scotland and settled in Kilkeel where he lived out his days in the local workhouse. Another of Kilkeel's sons was General Frances Chesney. He was the first person to survey the land between the Red Sea and the Mediterranean Sea and he concluded in 1830 that the construction of what became the Suez Canal was feasible. The canal was eventually built by Frenchman Ferdinand de Lesseps who referred to Chesney as the 'Pere du Canal' (Father of the Canal).

By now it was getting late in the evening and I wanted to finish the last part of the Mourne Coastal Route before dark. On the Kilkeel to Rostrevor road the wide expanse of Carlingford Lough and views of County Louth in the Republic of Ireland come into view. About half way along this road watch out for a sign to the Kilfeaghan Dolmen. This is an unusual tomb in that the stone that lies over the top is very big at 2.5 metres long and is estimated to weigh over 35 tonnes. This megalithic tomb is about 4,500 years old and has to be accessed via a farm.

Approaching Rostrevor the Mourne Mountains are close to the road again. Slieve Martin towers over the town and the forest covered slopes make for a picturesque setting that inspired the writer C.S. Lewis who once said 'That part of Rostrevor which overlooks Carlingford Lough is my idea of Narnia'. This part of County Down was a holiday destination for Lewis during his childhood, and I'm not surprised that this magical setting helped to inspire him to create his mythical Narnia. I parked the bike on the Shore Road leading into the town and walked along the short foreshore amenity area to drink in the stunning views. In the hills above Rostrevor there are many walks and trails that make this a popular destination for hikers. One of the curious things that you will see is a 30 tonne granite boulder, known locally as the 'Big Stone', on top of Slieve Martin. It was deposited here by retreating glaciers during the last Ice Age. A much more interesting explanation for how this rock got here comes from a legend that it was thrown by the giant Finn

McCool from the other side of Carlingford Lough during a battle to kill a rival giant called Ruscaire who was on the Rostrevor side of the Lough.

The Rostrevor Foreshore.

I noticed the sun setting over a tower in the distance and set off to see what it was. The 'tower' turned out to be a 30 metre tall granite obelisk erected in 1826 in memory of General Robert Ross who was born in Rostrevor in 1766. He was a General in the British Army and fought in both the Napoleonic Wars, and the War of 1812 between Britain and the United States. He is mostly known as the commander of British forces that burned Washington on 24 August 1814, in which the Presidential Mansion and the Capitol were set on fire. It is thought that the name now used for the Presidential Mansion, the White House, was given to the building after the fire when white paint was used to cover the scorch damage to the walls caused by Ross and his troops. The Ross Monument was restored in 2008 and is located near the spot where Ross had planned to build a retirement home on his return from war. Unfortunately he was not to see Rostrevor again as he was killed in a battle near Baltimore in 1815.

Narrow Water Castle, Warrenpoint.

There is just four kilometres the town of Rostrevor to the town of Warrenpoint, and the A2 road runs right along the shore between the two towns. By now Carlingford Lough narrows considerably before meeting the Newry River. The Republic of Ireland is just a few hundred metres away across the Lough, and can be reached via a short ferry trip to Omeath in County Louth. Warrenpoint is known as 'An Pointe' (meaning The Point) in the Irish language, and it is thought that the town's name is taken from the Waring family who lived here in the late eighteenth century. The long approach road into the town also features a footpath that makes for a popular promenade like walk for the locals and visiting tourists.

Just at the edge of Warrenpoint is the Narrow Water Castle National Monument where a lay-by provides ample parking for easy access. Castles of this type were built as command and control centres in strategic locations throughout Ireland between the fifteenth and early seventeenth centuries. The Narrow Water Castle dates from the 1560s and cost the princely sum of £361.4s.2d when it was built by John Sancky to protect Newry from attack from the sea. He became warder of the castle, a job that came with an annual salary of two shillings. This Narrow Water castle is not to be confused with another castle of the same name, the entrance which is directly across the road. This more modern version was built between 1816 and 1836 by Thomas Duff, an architect from nearby Newry, who also built several cathedrals in this part of Ireland including St Patrick's Cathedral in Armagh. Today the castle is home to the Hall family who have lived in this location since 1670 and it is also a popular venue for weddings. Right beside the entrance to the castle is the location where two explosions killed eighteen British soldiers on 27 August 1979. It's hard to stand here and imagine such death and destruction beside the peaceful and calm waters of Carlingford Lough.

I'm nearing the end of my journey and the dual carriageway from Warrenpoint quickly brings me to the last settlement on the Mourne Coastal Route: the City of Newry. It also marks the end of the A2 on which I started out on just a few days ago near Derry. Even with several detours I feel that my bike and I have now become roadie companions of the A2. Riding a motorcycle gives the rider a great feeling of closeness and attachment to the road, and having now travelled every kilometre of this road I would be sad to leave it. The A2 ends right in the centre of Newry and I decided to take a little time to explore this historic city.

Newcastle to Newry

Newry dates back to 1144 and is one of the oldest settlements in Ireland. Being close to the border with the Republic of Ireland, just six kilometres away, it has close ties with its hinterland to the south. Depending on the exchange rate between the euro and Sterling, the car parks of the shopping centres here, and accompanying traffic problems, can at times be full of southern registered cars. Newry is the fourth largest city in Northern Ireland and has being a gateway to and from the North and South of Ireland for centuries. Today it is a bustling shopping destination, but also has many places of interest for the touring visitor. In 2002 Newry was conferred with 'City' status as part of Queen Elizabeth II's Golden Jubilee.

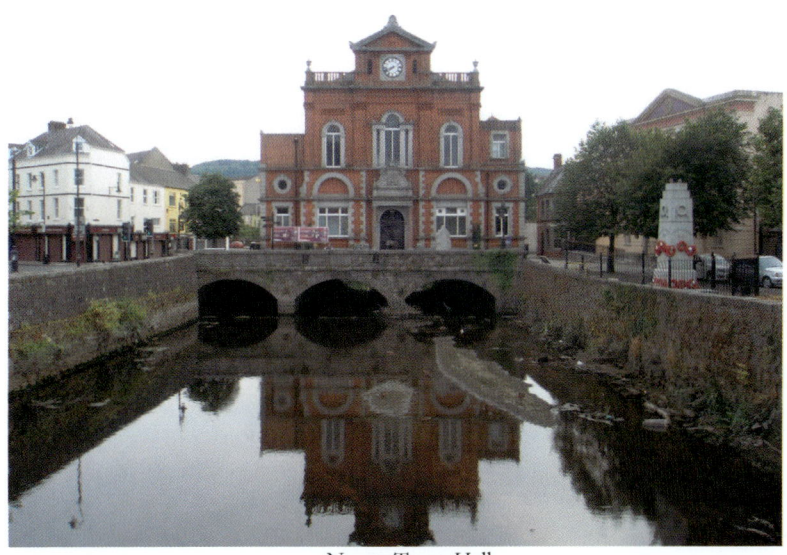

Newry Town Hall.

The Newry River splits the city into two sides and was the historic border between the counties of Armagh and Down. The classic-style Newry Town Hall is situated on three arches over the river. It is reputed that the Hall was built in 1893 like this, on the appropriately named 'Armaghdown Bridge', in the middle of the river to settle any rivalry between the people of Armagh and Down over which county it should be located in. Directly in front of the Town Hall is 'The Russian Trophy'. This is a cannon captured by the British from the Russians during the Crimean War and was presented to the town of Newry in recognition of the volunteers from the area who fought in the war. Beside the cannon is an interesting granite monument to Terence 'Banjo' Bannon documenting key moments in his ascent of Mount Everest in 2003. Bannon was born in Newry and is also the first local person to be conferred with the Freedom of the City of Newry.

Running alongside the Newry River is the Newry Canal which connects Carlingford Lough with Ireland's largest lake, Lough Neagh. It is the oldest canal in Britain or Ireland and was first built in 1741 to link coal fields in County Tyrone via the Irish Sea to Dublin. Despite many problems with water levels and lock construction the canal was navigable during the late eighteenth and early nineteenth centuries. It fell into decline in the 1850s with the coming of railways. It was still in use for small craft until it was abandoned in 1949. Today some parts are restored and it has become popular for coarse fishing, and the towpath beside the canal has been incorporated in the National Cycle Network.

Many signs on the approach roads to Newry invite visitors to see Bagenal's Castle, which is also the location for the Newry and Mourne Museum. Set overlooking the city, it was only rediscovered in 1996 as it was until then enclosed by a bakery. Now restored to part of its former glory it is a flagship project for the local council. Fortunately the restoration was assisted by having the original plans of the castle, dating from 1568, in the National Archives of the United Kingdom. The castle is named after Nicholas Bagenal who in 1550 was given a lease of a house in Newry, the Bagenal family lived here until 1712. By 1570 a map which still exists shows a new castle which is believed to be the beginnings of what still exists today. In the early 1800s the site was first used as residences and shops. In 1804 the site was purchased by Arthur McCann who converted it to a bakery. It was only when the bakery was sold that the castle was rediscovered and restored. The Newry and Mourne Museum features many galleries and exhibitions detailing the heritage and growth of Newry.

Just like in Warrenpoint, Newry has its own obelisk. The Corry Monument is located near the centre of the city and is dedicated to Trevor Corry who served with 'integrity, ability, and virtue' as a magistrate here for 35 years. The Obelisk was erected to his memory in

1877 by the 'Inhabitants of Newry'. Another Newry native with the same name is commemorated in St Mary's Church in the town centre. Sir Trevor Corry was a diplomat who served mainly with distinction as Consul representing the British King in Poland during the Seven Years' War (1754-1763). In honour of his service he was confirmed with the title of 'Baron to the Throne of Poland' by the Polish King in 1773, and he was knighted by King George III in 1776. In his will he left £1,000 for the development of St Mary's Church, and £3,000 for the poor of Newry. Directly across the road from St Mary's is a statue of John Mitchel who was a leading member of the Young Irelander movement in the mid-nineteenth century and who spent his early life here. His most famous work is the book 'Jail Journal' about when he was transported to Van Dieman's Land for his rebellious activities in 1848. In total he spent 27 years in exile and returned to live in Newry where he died in 1875. There are many other interesting sites in the city which can be visited on the Newry Heritage Trail.

Bagenal's Castle, Newry.

Exploring Northern Ireland's Causeway and Mourne Coastal Routes

By now it was starting to get dark and it was time to ride home to Dublin. In just four days I had travelled almost 500 kilometres around both the Causeway and Mourne Coastal Routes. I had met friendly people and seen sights I had never been to before. As always on a trip like this that hugs the coastline, there are inestimable wonders inland from the coast that I had seen many signs for, but passed by to explore on another day. Exploring the Causeway and Mourne Coastal Routes is a great way to see Northern Ireland. Another motorcycle odyssey awaits to explore the heart of this beautiful country.

Exploring Northern Ireland's Causeway and Mourne Coastal Routes

Eugene O'Loughlin

Sources

A Guide to the Glens of Antrim. (http://www.discovernorthernireland.com/attachment.aspx?attachmentID=1233)

Abandoned Ireland. (http://www.abandonedireland.com)

Annalong. (http://www.annalong.com)

Antrim Coasts & Glens. (http://antrimcoastandglensaonb.ccght.org)

Ask About Ireland. (http://www.askaboutireland.ie)

BBC Northern Ireland. (http://www.bbc.co.uk/northernireland)

Belfast City Council. (http://www.belfastcity.gov.uk)

Belfast Grand Opera House. (http://www.goh.co.uk/history-heritage)

Belfast History - 100 Years of a Journey. (http://www.belfasthistory.net)

Belfast Telegraph. (http://www.belfasttelegraph.co.uk)

Bogside Artists. (http://www.bogsideartists.com)

Carlingford & Mourne. (http://www.carlingfordandmourne.com)

Carrickfergus Borough Council. (http://www.carrickfergus.org)

Castles in Ireland. (http://www.castlesinireland.com)

Castles of the World. (http://www.castles.org)

Exploring Northern Ireland's Causeway and Mourne Coastal Routes

Causeway Coastal Route. (http://www.causewaycoastalroute.com)

Causeway Coastal Route Alive. (http://ccralive.com)

Causeway Coast Way. (http://www.causewaycoastway.com)

Cloughey & District Community Association. (http://www.cloughey.org.uk)

Coleraine Borough Council. (http://www.colerainebc.gov.uk)

Comber Historical Society. (http://www.comberhistory.com)

Continental Road Trip. (https://www.continentalroadtrip.com)

Crumlin Road Gaol. (http://www.crumlinroadgaol.com)

Derry City Council. (http://www.derrycity.gov.uk)

Derry Journal. (http://www.derryjournal.com)

Discover Ireland. (http://www.discoverireland.ie)

Discovering Ireland. (http://www.discoveringireland.com)

Discover Northern Ireland. (http://www.discovernorthernireland.com)

Down County Museum. (http://www.downcountymuseum.com)

Encyclopedia Titanica (http://www.encyclopedia-titanica.org)

Exploris - The Northern Ireland Aquarium. (http://www.exploris.org.uk)

Geneology.com (http://www.genealogy.com)

Geographical Sites in Northern Ireland. (http://www.habitas.org.uk)

Sources

Geography in Action. (http://www.geographyinaction.co.uk)

Greyabbey Community Web Site. (http://www.greyabbey.com)

Groomsport Village Association. (http://www.groomsport.info)

Independent Review of Foot and Mouth Disease in Northern Ireland. (http://www.crossborder.ie/pubs/fmdclar.pdf)

In Your Footsteps. (http://www.inyourfootsteps.com)

Ireland Now – Castles and Shamrocks. (http://irelandnow.com)

Ireland's History in Maps. (http://www.rootsweb.ancestry.com)

Irish Archaeology. (http://www.irisharchaeology.ie)

Irish Masonic History and the Jewels of Irish Freemasonry. (http://www.irishmasonichistory.com)

Irish Wrecks On-line. (http://www.irishwrecksonline.net)

Joyce, P.W., Sullivan, A.M., Nunan, P.D. (1900). *Atlas and Cyclopedia of Ireland*. New York: Murphy & McCarthy.

Kilkeel. (http://www.kilkeel.info)

Kircubbin Community Church. (http://www.kircomchu.com)

Kirkistown Motor Racing Circuit. (http://www.kirkistown.com)

Larne Borough Council. (http://www.larne.gov.uk)

Library Ireland. (http://www.libraryireland.com)

Limavady Borough Council. (http://www.limavady.gov.uk)

Lord Belmont in Northern Ireland.
(http://lordbelmontinnorthernireland.blogspot.ie)

Megalithic Ireland. (http://www.megalithicireland.com)

Mourne Cooley Gullion Geotourism.
(http://www.mournecooleygullion.com)

Mourne Mountains & Ring of Gullion.
(http://www.visitmournemountains.co.uk)

Narrow Water Castle. (http://www.narrowwatercastle.ie)

National Association for AONBs. (http://www.aonb.org.uk)

National Historic Ships UK. (http://www.nationalhistoricships.org.uk)

National Museums Northern Ireland. (http://www.nmni.com)

Newry and Mourne District Council. (http://newryandmourne.gov.uk)

Newry and Mourne Museum. (http://www.bagenalscastle.com)

North Down Borough Council Tourism.
(http://www.northdowntourism.com)

Northern Ireland Environment Agency. (http://www.doeni.gov.uk)

Northern Ireland's North Coast Visitor Guide. (www.northcoastni.com)

Ordinance Survey Ireland (2012). *Official Road Atlas Ireland*.

Portaferry Online. (http://www.portaferry.info)

Portaferry Parish. (http://www.portaferryparish.com)

Saints and Stones. (http://www.saintsandstones.net)

Sources

Saint Patrick Centre. (http://www.saintpatrickcentre.com)

Scrabo Tower Web Portal. (http://scrabotower.com)

Sea Generation Limited. (http://www.seageneration.co.uk)

Stones & Thrones. (http://www.stonesandthrones.com)

Strangford Lough & Lecale Partnership. (http://www.strangfordlough.org)

The Gems of Antrim. (http://www.thegemsofantrim.com)

The Glens of Antrim Historical Society. (http://www.antrimhistory.net)

The Great War 1914 - 1918. (http://www.greatwar.co.uk)

The Guardian Newspaper. (http://www.theguardian.com)

The Lecale Peninsula. (http://lecalepeninsula.wordpress.com)

The Man Who Captured Washington. (http://www.themanwhocapturedwashington.com)

The National Trust. (http://www.nationaltrust.org.uk)

The Old Inn Crawfordsburn. (http://www.theoldinn.com)

The Orange Order. (http://www.grandorangelodge.co.uk)

The Royal British Legion. (http://www.britishlegion.org.uk)

Titanic Quarter. (http://www.titanic-quarter.com)

Tracing your Mourne Roots. (http://www.tracingyourmourneroots.com)

111

Railway Preservation Society of Ireland.
(http://www.steamtrainsireland.com)

Ulster Architectural Heritage Society. (http://www.uahs.org.uk)

Ulster Journal of Archaeology.
(http://www.jstor.org/action/showPublication?journalCode=ulstjarch)

Ulster Scots Heritage Trail. (http://ulsterscotstrail.com)

Ulster War Memorials. (http://www.ulsterwarmemorials.net)

Visit Belfast. (http://visit-belfast.com)

Visit Derry. (http://www.visitderry.com)

Visit Donaghadee. (http://www.visitdonaghadee.com)

Visit Kilkeel. (http://www.visitkilkeel.com)

Visit Strangford Lough. (http://www.visitstrangfordlough.co.uk)

Walk Northern Ireland. (http://www.walkni.com)

Wonderful Ireland. (http://www.wonderfulireland.ie)

World War II in Northern Ireland.
(http://thesneakybandit.com/wwiini)

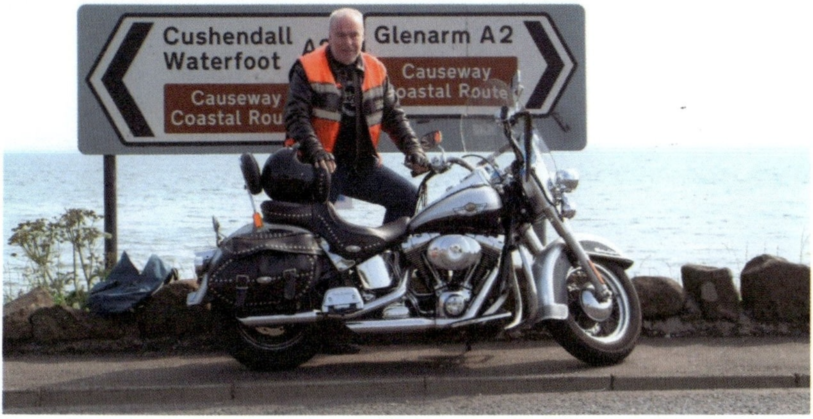

Cushendall
Waterfoot
Glenarm A2
Causeway
Causeway

Printed in Great
Britain
by Amazon